Developing Nursery
Education

Innovations in Education

Series Editor: Colin Fletcher (Lecturer in the School of Policy Studies, Cranfield Institute of Technology)

There have been periods of major innovation in public education. What do the achievements amount to and what are the prospects for progress now? There are issues in each slice of the education sector. How have the issues come about?

Each author analyses their own sphere, argues from experience and communicates clearly. Here are books that speak both with and for the teaching profession; books that can be shared with all those involved in the future of education.

Three quotations have helped to shape the series:

> The whole process – the false starts, frustrations, adaptions, the successive recasting of intentions, the detours and conflicts – needs to be comprehended. Only then can we understand what has been achieved and learn from experience.
>
> *Marris and Rein*

> In this time of considerable educational change and challenge the need for teachers to write has never been greater.
>
> *Hargreaves*

> A wise innovator should prepare packages of programmes and procedures which . . . could be put into effect quickly in periods of recovery and reorganisation following a disaster.
>
> *Hirsh*

CURRENT TITLES IN THE SERIES

Developing Nursery Education:
from conflicts towards cooperation

Julia Gilkes

Open University Press

Milton Keynes · Philadelphia

Open University Press
Open University Educational Enterprises Limited
12 Cofferidge Close
Stony Stratford
Milton Keynes MK11 1BY, England

and

242 Cherry Street
Philadelphia, PA 19106, USA

First published 1987

British Library Cataloguing in Publication Data

Gilkes, Julia
  Developing nursery education: from
  conflicts towards cooperation.—
  (Innovations in education).
  1. Education, Preschool—Great Britain
  I. Title   II. Series
  372'.27'0941   LB1140.25.G7

ISBN 0 335 10284 0

ISBN 0 335 10283 2 Pbk

Library of Congress Cataloging in Publication Data

Gilkes, Julia
  Developing nursery education
  1. Nursery schools—Great Britain.   I. Title
  LB1140.25.G7G55 1987   372'. 216'0941   87–7631

ISBN 0–335–10284–0

ISBN 0–335–10283–2 (Pbk)

Text design by Clarke Williams
Typeset by S & S Press, Abingdon, Oxfordshire
Printed in Great Britain by
Thomson Litho Ltd, East Kilbride, Scotland

Contents

Series editor's foreword

Nursery education is beset by major problems. The words of enabling legislation are weak and woolly – the result is provision for some under fives and bitter competition "to get children in". Close co-operation is needed between social services, education and health. But these agencies are usually huge bureaucracies with an imperial disdain towards their far-flung colonies, the nurseries themselves. At the same time great skill is needed to work with the very young and their parents. Yet these skills draw from contrasting disciplines such as psychology, medicine and community work. Furthermore, every time there are cut backs, nursery education, is exposed to sacrifice. Through its image of being 'women's work' there is an unrestrained chauvinism in private whilst it lacks powerful friends in public.

Yet despite all these obstacles, there are real successes. Some centres cut through the red tape and thrive. Kirkby Nursery Centre's story shows what is humanly and sensibly possible. All day long there is the light and shade of working with parents, resting and playing, eating and exercising both within the "baby den" and all around with the "older ones". In comparison the building was designed like a filing cabinet with each activity to be safely and securely slotted away. However, fullest possible use is made of a shared space right up to the limits of the outside walls.

When something is working well we usually want to know how its parts fit together and pull in the same direction. Julia Gilkes shows that co-operation comes from recognizing the real conflicts within almost every aspect of nursery education. She organizes this book by saying what the conflicts are, how they appear and are felt at Kirkby. Then she shows how they were overcome by the dedication of all participants.

The heart of this book is an unfolding story about a place and its people; the town, staff, parents and children are described in the events of the day and on outings. Each chapter is self-contained as it gets to grips with a set of issues. The issues are clearly expressed but never laboured – from who should be admitted to becoming a community resource, from the transitions into school to embarking on staff development – until the account is complete.

Developing Nursery Education is unique because the author does not put all her faith into any one argument. Each issue gets full attention. She has also written equally for nursery nurses, teachers, parents and administrators. The openess and scrupulous fairness will surprise, delight and dismay them all. The reader is led to realize again and again what enjoyable and difficult work it can be. This careful and honest account of Kirkby Centre steps beyond the conflicts to reach the co-operation which can be achieved. The author drives towards her concluding ideals for nursery education – from which come the criteria for a national policy.

Colin Fletcher

Acknowledgements

This book is about a wonderful experience. It has been a privilege to be part of an educational adventure. I would therefore like to acknowledge the work of all the Kirkby Centre staff in making this book possible. I would like readers to be aware of the hard work of the earliest staff before I arrived as Head of Centre. We all built on their experience and learning. However, the most rewarding part of the years at Kirkby are attributed to my dear friends and colleagues, Coreen Brookes and Daphne Carré. Their commitment, trust and professionalism created a truly satisfying partnership.

Many colleagues in the area contributed to the success of the Centre. These include Pam and Trevor Lewis, Jackie Combes who, with the Social Work team, the Health Visitors and Probation provided endless support and encouragement.

Our families created a unique opportunity to try new approaches to supporting family life. The children were always at the centre of our vision for a nursery which could truly be called a community resource.

Finally, my love and thanks to Horace, Sarah and Daniel who have given me such a fulfilled and exciting family life.

Introduction

This personal account of the early work experienced in a newly established combined nursery centre will, I hope, contribute to the continuing debate for more effective pre-school provision for children and support for their families. Whilst recalling those early years, it is pleasing to know that the learning experienced and the skills developed by the staff have been acknowledged in a number of reports and council debates and were included in the local Labour Party Manifesto. There have been changes in the day nurseries with teacher and community liaison posts and the development of Family Centres. However there has been little development in nursery classes and schools to provide more flexibility for families. There is a great need for the teachers unions to recognise a more flexible approach towards nursery teachers' conditions of service if close cooperation with Social Services is to work. We will then begin to tackle the cycle of deprivation more effectively.

Until the changing needs of families with young children are fully acknowledged by the education system, traditional nursery education will continue to make a limited contribution to the development of young children. Research studies and eminent professors from University Departments have pointed to the essential links between health, education and social service workers. This account aims to share the practicalities of this liaison and the benefits for the child and the family, with the enrichment of the nursery staff practice.

I visited a nursery class in an infant school recently in an area with poor housing, litter and filth around, the coal tip looming behind the playground and children and adults looking pale and poorly clad. The nursery had 40 children each morning and each afternoon with three staff. The facilities were designed for the very young child, with little thought for the need for parents to share the experience. Many children had an air of physical neglect, with poor speech and language skills. Many had delayed intellectual development and suffered from a number of minor health problems. In their family life there was a high incidence of obesity, marital stress, violence and ill health. The community room in the school (a spare classroom) was a lifeline to many parents. Yet the needs of these children are barely met in spite of the commitment of the excellent staff. The Department of Education and Science ratio of 1–13 adult to pupils is totally inadequate in this type of community. Nursery staff are working with parents, speech therapists, police, social workers, health visitors, paediatricians and their own school colleagues. Although trying to offer a flexible programme to children and flexible attendance hours for parents, it is quite unjust to expect 3 staff to work consistently throughout a day with up to 70–80 children, their parents and key workers, and also to develop links within the school and care for children throughout the lunch hour.

This book is about resources to meet the changing patterns in the care and education of young children. Here is the evidence of changing attitudes, developing new skills and sharing expertise. We cannot go on exploiting the nursery staffs throughout the country by acknowledging the demands and expectations made on them without coordinating the resources, increasing the staffing and expanding the training opportunities to equip them more appropriately for the job, and offering them a realistic salary.

Julia Gilkes
April 1986

CHAPTER 1

Conflicts in the education and care of the pre-school child

What do parents need?

During the last twenty five years there has been a steady flow of literature on the early years of childhood. Surveys, research and changes in government policies and local authority responsibilities have provided an opportunity for close examination and reflection of existing provision and new approaches to meeting family and child need. Some interesting reports have emerged from professional associations, unions, universities, local authorities and government departments and the voluntary agencies.

Pre-school workers have received much advice during this time. Changes in their attitudes, role and expertise have been taking place and it is necessary to share their practical experience and add it to the continuing flow of academic guidance which many mainstream pre-school workers rarely read or have access to.

Britain has no centralised, free, comprehensive nursery provision and a wide range of services has emerged. Parents' choice depends greatly on availability in the area or district in which the family lives and whether the provision is free or fee paying. Pre-school provision may be available through the local Education Department, the Social Services Department, or a bewildering spread of voluntary agencies, for example playgroups and childminding. There are different philosophies, facilities, expectations and experience throughout this range. Many parents have to accept, or look elsewhere or do without. In some cases they have created their own provision.

These restrictions are frustrating to families as often their choice of pre-school provision is not flexible enough to meet the family need. A survey of families in a small mining town in Nottinghamshire who were using a nursery centre gives some useful insights into family needs and requests for a nursery place.

First, parents wanted a safe and caring place, easily accessible so that the mother could work, whether she was single and coping on her own or living with a partner. Most parents also felt that enquiries into their everyday life was an invasion of privacy, insulting and no business of 'the authorities'. If they had made the decision to work, for whatever the reason, then a place at the nursery should be available. The positive discrimination for social priority cases established in Social Services day nurseries promotes much discord in a close community. Many times a distressed parent would scream in the nursery office, 'Do I have to batter my kids before you give me a nursery place?' or 'Do I have to leave my husband before I get on the list?' Tremendous anger and rejection may occur in a street where families are patiently or despairingly waiting for a nursery place and then a newcomer rehoused next door is offered a place immediately. Nevertheless some families so rejected were in great need.

One of the most common requests was for some relief from the exhausting every day care of young children. Some requests were for several months full day care to support the parents who were not coping and were quite distressed, tense, tired and sometimes despairing of ever returning to a calm, normal living existence. Others were requests for relief from everyday child care. This was regularly sought for two year olds. Many mothers found this age the most demanding and exhausting and if they had little support from family or friends turned to the nursery for relief. Such a request often identified a family with several young children under the age of five. There was a high number of families with three pre-school children, and some with four and five, or at least four or five under the age of six years. The need for part-time places was, in many cases, to give the mother more time with a new baby or to shop without three young children in the pram or taken on the bus with a buggy and baskets.

An increasing number of parents find childrearing very demanding and difficult. Their expectations of early childhood development are often quite unrealistic; for example, toilet trained by eighteen months. Excessive bedwetting, feeding problems, handicap, delayed development, behaviour problems and so on can contribute to breakdown in the parent–child relationship. Personal support, praise and encouragement is essential for the new or struggling parent. If the family and community are not providing this support the nursery can offer such sympathy, guidance and relief. Many places at the nursery were taken to catch hold of a helping hand.

Another significant need emerged in the community within its stable extended families. Parents with young children could well be also supporting their brothers and sisters or other relatives, and, of course, one or both parents and even grandparents. The nursery centre was in a mining community where depressive illnesses, alcohol abuse, along with mining diseases and accidents often added extra burdens to adult members of the family. A place at the nursery several days a week offered many women a respite from their children to give them time to care for their other relatives.

The high percentage of marital breakdown even in families with pre-school children was great and saddening. At one time 56 children out of a total of 98 were not living with both natural parents. Many requests for nursery places were made to give the single parent time to adjust to marital breakdown, or to spend time sorting it out. A number of young mothers had tragically died from incurable diseases. Young fathers needed time to adjust and decide whether to continue work or take on full-time childcare. Others needed the places immediately in order to continue to work. Further requests were made to support women whose husbands were in prison, some with fifteen year sentences. Violence, personal abuse and the fear of a partner resulted in some requests for places to know their children would not witness their parents' physical abuses.

Lastly, many requests were made for a nursery place so that the parent, mostly women of course, but increasingly the single male parent, could have some time to themselves. In the womens' movement this time is commonly known as 'personal space', time to be 'me' to do what I want, released from commitments to family and job. Most men claim this time as their right. Many are totally unsympathetic to the young mothers' right for personal space and accuse them of selfishness.

This review of a number of families with young children in a small community and their pressing needs has not mentioned at all the parents' hopes for the child at the nursery. In most cases families had some vague hope or knowledge that the nursery would 'do' something for the child. (This will be developed in depth at a later stage).

The conflict which immediately arises is that parents have different immediate personal needs, and have changing requirements in the upbringing of their young children particularly those which are related to the child's stages of development. Mothers, in particular, are caught in a net of guilt and anxiety. Society has led most young mothers to expect a rewarding, exciting, natural fulfilment in motherhood, homemaking and taking care of a working husband. The reality for many mothers with young children is exhausting physical work in the home with the constant expectation that they shall be available to any member of the family. Many mothers suffer confusion and anxiety with the first baby whilst learning by doing; they are often unsupported suffering personal isolation and a dramatic drop in everyday adult contact with a reduction in intellectual challenge. From the end of the 1970s, unemployment was to affect the expectation of a family having a male breadwinner. For many of this nursery's mothers the 'twilight' shift and homework connected with the hosiery, underwear and childrens wear industry was essential to support out-of-work husbands or those with low incomes. Many families existed around shift systems for both or one partner.

What is provided?

In any given area the range of pre-school provision does not often reflect the range of parental need. The private or workplace day nursery and the private childminder provide care for young children on a daily basis whilst their parents are at work. The private day nursery will be open for long hours which does offer scope for children to attend at differing hours around the parent's work and travelling time. This provision is a straightforward business contract which can be very expensive. The day nursery may be also a long distance from the child's home and/or the parent's workplace. Usually the staff are lower paid than the local authority nurseries and have little training and no opportunity for further training. Many single parents and those with low income cannot afford this expensive facility. The childminder may be more locally based, perhaps even a neighbour.

Childminding is an old profession. Women have helped other women with the care of their children for reward for many, many years. In 1948, following the closure of so many wartime nurseries, there was still a great demand for day care for young children. The Nurseries and Childminders Act 1948, amended 1968, required local authorities to register and inspect the homes of women wishing to care for pre-school children in their own homes for more than two hours for reward. During the 1970s, following Brian Jackson's exposure of the often poor care of the children and the exploitation of the registered and unregistered minder, it became clear that there was a need for more frequent inspection, constructive training and support for the minders. The emergence of the National Childminding Association has quite rightly set standards of pay at an appropriate level for the work involved to reduce exploitation of the low paid home worker. Childminding, again, will be too expensive for many although the flexibility and home base for young children is very desirable. The advantages of this provision for many parents are that 'officials' are not prying into private lives; meanstesting, using discriminatory criteria (on social deprivation, neglect or incompetence) for admission or suggesting that only part-time provision is available and thus implying disapproval if full-time places are requested.

The local playgroups, of course, offer in many cases superb opportunities for parents and children to share in local exchanges. The ideals of the movement, that parents can enjoy and learn together through play, through sharing experiences with other families and the superb opportunities for continuing education for the parents, in particular the mothers, is something to hold dear to any pre-school organisation philosophy. In fact it reflects Margaret McMillan's original philosophy when setting up the Deptford nurseries earlier in the century. One of her goals on setting up a nursery school in the East End of London had been to help parents improve their child rearing practices and to develop their own potential. She recognised the loss of opportunity for change if parents were not closely involved in their child's early education and unaware of their child's needs and development. She also recognised the growth in personal esteem of parents encouraged to embark in a partnership with the staff and their involvement in clubs and workshops.

However, there are many families who could never take part in the life of the local playgroup. There are fees to pay, funds to raise, time to give to the organisation and a rather ordered life that can get children to the group early and collect them on time and only requires two or three half sessions each week. Within playgroups themselves there is often a great turnover of staff and many staff with little training. They are closed during school holidays. Their closure at these times excludes the working parent(s) and, also in most cases, the family trying to cope with severe demands, the low income group, the handicapped and depressed mother, the parent with children under the age of three years.

In some areas parents will have the choice of a nursery school or a class staffed by trained teachers and nursery nurses. There is no statutory responsibility to provide them and thus in some authorities provision is well developed, in others non-existent. Places are offered mostly on a part-time basis. Mrs Thatcher's White Paper 'A Framework for Expansion' followed the Plowden Committee's recommendations that nursery education should be available either for a morning or an afternoon session for five days a week. Only 15% per cent of children could expect a full day place. Plowden recommends that a low priority should be given to mothers who could not satisfy the authorities that they had exceptionally good reasons to work. This recommendation has created one of the most damaging conflicts in relationships between teachers, nursery nurses and parents. Teachers pride themselves that their priorities are centred on the needs of children in their care. Their responsibilities are to create a suitable learning environment with appropriate concern for children's safety and health.

The headteacher or the teacher in charge of a nursery class starts off badly as most initial discussions open with arguments over there being only part-time places 'unless there are exceptional circumstances'. For most families, the circumstances are exceptional and individual to them. Parents naturally feel capable of making decisions for their children so much anger and resentment evolves from any policy that teachers, social workers, educational welfare officers and so on should determine whether parents have the right to receive a full-time nursery place for their children.

The opportunity of a free part-time place at the nursery class is frequently not taken up by families with severe problems. The 2–2½ hours is too short to have any meaning for the family. In fact it creates more problems as the parent has to fetch and deliver the child in such a short time. Once more the school holidays close the nurseries, so that some families beginning to develop a routine flounder back into disorder.

The most notable difference which has emerged is that nursery education is free of charge, just as the education and care of the five year old in the primary or infant school is. For many parents there is confusion and conflict about the policy in one neighbourhood school which admits four year olds full-time into an infant class the term after their fourth birthday, with a school meal at midday and the school nearby with a nursery class offering only a morning or afternoon session with no meals 'unless in exceptional circumstances'.

This further conflict has established itself, particularly in the 1980s, regarding the admission of 4 year olds into statutory schooling. As falling rolls in schools have created many problems for education authorities, one convenient way of stabilising school numbers has been to admit children into school in the term of their fourth birthday, often with only an annual intake. The free, full day place with a hot midday meal and a good 'start' to formal schooling seems to meet the demands of many parents regardless of the needs of the child. Children are finding themselves in classes with 4–8 year olds in small village communities, in 4–7 year classes in vertically grouped schools and in pre-admission classes for one, two or three terms. Their teachers are frequently untrained in the earliest years of education, rarely have ancillary staff or nursery nurse colleagues in the classroom and the curriculum and classroom organisation is often unsuitable for the young child. Parents will inevitably be even less involved in their child's early education in this school setting.

The last type of provision in the conflict-ridden pre-school field is the day nursery funded by Social Services Departments. Once again there is no statutory requirement to provide them and many authorities have very few. The staff are now usually trained nursery nurses but in the 1950s and 1960s many staff were trained nurses, i.e., trained to deal with sick people. This nursery does cater for young babies as well as the toddler and the growing 3–5 year old. Most day nurseries in the 1960s and early 1970s were admitting children from families with a number of social difficulties and stresses identified in the Seebohm report that led to the setting up of the Social Services Departments. The nurseries then emerged from the strict, hygiene and passive care of the Health Department towards a preventative social work resource to support parents in difficulty and as a safe place for 'abused' and 'at risk' children. The criteria for admission was on the recommendation of a professional worker with means tested fees in most cases. The newly formed Social Services Departments were to give priority to those with a special need; these may include children of lone working parents, children with a mental or physical handicap, those whose home environment is so socially impoverished or so strained that day care is considered necessary for their welfare and whose parents are, through illness or handicap, unable to look after them during the day. Although open 50 weeks of the year, and for a full day, admission is rarely possible for the ordinary working parent. Thus many parents with difficulties can have had their feelings of inadequacy deepened, were rarely involved in the nursery with their children and were almost always offered a full-time place. As it is such a scarce resource it has become available to a very disadvantaged minority.

The need for change

There is little data available on the demand and need for daycare services before the 1970s. The tables in the Plowden report relate to take up of services for children aged 2–5 years, (it does not clarify the position for those under two years). The Government and Social Survey evidence suggested that 21 per cent of women likely to return to work planned to use nurseries but did not show 21 per cent of non-working women who had not considered which arrangements they might wish to make. Nor did the report take into consideration the 84 per cent who said day nurseries and nursery schools were too far away, too expensive or had unsuitable hours or that it was too difficult to get in.

These points suggest that a considerable number of mothers of pre-school children would have taken advantage of a well planned service of group care facilities if one had been available.

Eric Midwinter and A. H. Halsey were commissioned to look closely at Education Priority Areas in the 1960s. They produced evidence of the need for more resources, closer involvement with the families and the effects of poverty on young children's education.

Tessa Blackstone's research into daycare and education also revealed the changing patterns in the States which could be adjusted to meet British needs. She recognised that the traditional view that the family is the only legitimate child rearing agency is breaking down. She suggested the expansion of day nurseries, a family day-care service, integrating education care for under fives, large scale encouragement of genuine parental involvement in pre-school institutions, universally available nursery education.

In 1974 there were two interesting surveys into the need for day care. The Office of Population Censuses and Surveys survey was used to help the D.H.S.S. formulate policy guidelines for local authorities and used the Seebohm criteria of social need. A random sample of 2500 families were selected. The Thomas Coram Research Unit also carried out a local survey amongst a random sample of 350 mothers in a small catchment area of two nurseries in London. The evidence produced by both the national and local surveys was very similar and provided a clear comment from families that part-time nursery expansion as recommended by Plowden and by the White Paper was not wanted. Sixty four per cent of all families with children under 1 year to 5 years desired some form of day care, 87 per cent of families with 3 year olds desired it as did 91 per cent with 4 year olds. A startling element in the surveys revealed that 46 per cent of families with 2 year olds required some form of nursery provision.

Only 20 per cent of families with children aged 0–5 wished for 3–4 hour sessional places. Fifteen per cent required 5–6 hour placements and 24 per cent required more than 7 hours. Once more the two year old group were highlighted. Twenty three per cent of families required a placement for 3–4 hours for their 2 year old and an unexpected 34 per cent required more than 7 hours. It seems that less than 10 per cent of the mothers in the Thomas Coram survey would *choose* a nursery open less than 3 hours.

Thus the seeds were sown to re-examine some of the fundamental philosophies of early childhood education and day care. Jack Tizard stated at an important conference at Sunningdale in 1976 that 'expansion could best take place through the development of integrated nursery centres offering medical services, education and full or part-time day care as desired by parents, with parental participation and involvement'. Mia Kellmer Pringle commented at the Sunningdale conference in 1976 that the aim of nursery centres would be to eliminate and minimise the potential shortcomings and pool the advantages of each type of provision. She suggested that the centre would provide a more comprehensive programme for each child, balancing physical care, mothering, stimulation, child directed exploration and adult guided learning according to individual need and provide activities for mothers themselves.

The core of this book is a personal account of the development of the Kirkby Nursery Centre. It includes personal comments from staff and parents. Pre-school workers in the statutory and voluntary sectors will recognise many of their own conflicts and experiences. It is hoped that this account will reassure and reinvigorate them, will cause a smile or two and perhaps remember a tear shed in the name of pre-school progress.

Summary of the conflicts

1 The divisive separation of establishments which provide care or education for young children.
2 A free comprehensive pre-school service available to all families who require it or a limited piecemeal provision relying on local priorities and initiatives.
3 An appropriately trained pre-school staff skilled in working with adults and children and particularly committed to parent partnership as opposed to lowering the age of statutory schooling for convenience without adequate resources.
4 Interagency and departmental co-operation to provide a quality service for the needs of the whole child.
5 Parent substitution or parental participation.
6 The role of the nursery teacher and other pre-school staff.

CHAPTER 2

Kirkby Nursery Centre – changing attitudes, roles and expectations

> Whenever a serious change in socialisation and educational practices is about to be introduced into a society, a debate commences between the advocates of reform and those who fear the change because it challenges their ideology   Clarkson Stewart and Fein. (1973)

There is no blueprint for creating and managing change. The early years of development at the Centre were stressful, challenging and full of new learning, for the staff, the families and colleagues in the community.

The recent research and national encouragement of integrating the pre-school services provided a way forward towards establishing our aims to break the cycle of deprivation. A commitment to co-operate and liaise effectively with health and social work colleagues, required time and new communication skills. Creating a useful dialogue with the two departments funding the Centre offered a new experience in working with administration, the advisory network and local politicians. Throughout those early years the high turnover of Centre staff created its own problems in management, staff development and team building.

The establishment of a new combined centre at Kirkby was courageous and imaginative because of the potential it had to offer the children and families, and the benefits of its location on the same site as a new primary school and school for children with moderate and severe learning difficulties. Unfortunately it was not central to the town so that one of the old council estates with poorer accommodation and a larger number of families rehoused there with social problems was not in easy pram-pushing distance of the centre. There was a Health Centre with five Health Visitors nearby and a local Social Services office served the town and was easily accessible to the staff, and parents with a car, but for many parents was a short bus ride away.

The town had little to offer the young child in terms of safe play space out of doors and free pre-school facilities were almost non existent. There were three playgroups established in the early 1970s. One nursery class was built onto an infant school and there were no registered childminders. Occasionally a few mothers had registered, but very quickly gave up the job. There was a private day nursery in a nearby village and a work-place nursery at a knitwear factory some distance away. Both day nurseries provided transport included in the weekly fees.

What was new?

The centre was purpose built to integrate 80 children aged from six weeks to 5 years plus, offering flexible hours of attendance between 8 a.m. and 6 p.m. for 50 weeks of the year. Breakfast, lunch and tea are available. The challenges for developing the centre were many. Some were educational and social priorities for the child and parent, other essential challenges were to support staff through innovations and changes as the centre became established as a family resource.

The areas for innovation and change

1 Respecting, adapting and combining differing early childhood philosophies and practice, this included the differing expectations of parents, teachers, nursery nurses, health visitors and social workers.
2 The essential element for change was to offer some choice, some understanding of why the choice was there, and an expectation that parents realised that choices could change as need arose. For example, the family coping with a crisis receiving

a full-time place could change to less nursery time as pressure diminished. The family coping well with life might experience unexpected trauma due to death or divorce or redundancy. The part-time place could be increased to more nursery time. Providing flexible patterns of attendance presented an unexpected disturbance in the staff. The challenge was to change existing practice and planning for more individual and indepth learning experience. Flexibility meant much more work for staff as well as significant change in nursery nurse attitudes. Many nurses believed full day care was more desirable as it reduced any disruption or disturbance to the child's routine.

3 Creating more effective consultation and communication patterns between staff, parents and other agencies.
4 Fostering confidence and an expectation of a partnership which included friendship between professional and parent.
5 Developing the strengths of the staff who had very different training. This included raising the morale and esteem of nursery nurses as well as encouraging all staff to respect each other as true committed professionals.
6 Creating a community resource and network of expertise and knowledge to support families with young children.
7 Sharing facilities with parents and voluntary agencies and to co-operate and work together for the benefit of the community.

This provision could change Sir Keith Joseph's cycle of deprivation into a cycle of opportunity for both parents and children as seen in Figure 2.1

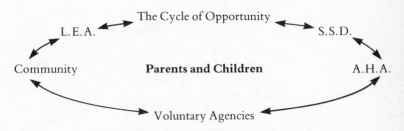

Figure 2.1 The Cycle of Opportunity

Here was a unique opportunity to talk and listen to parents and other professionals, to share and try out ideas, to challenge some repressive practices and to seek many types of support to enrich and nurture the mostly young staff in an exciting new experience.

The neighbourhood

Kirkby is essentially a mining town which developed in the late nineteenth century and early twentieth century from a small village of attractive local stone cottages surrounding the village church into a sprawling town with council estates, Coal Board terraced housing, a hotpotch of private housing, a colliery and a range of small industries related to knitwear and light engineering. As the town developed it absorbed smaller hamlets and joined the developing town of Sutton-in-Ashfield. The result is a sprawling built up area of Kirkby, Kirkby Woodhouse and Annesley leading into Sutton and eventually Mansfield. There are still some small farmhouses in the town with some agricultural development surviving on the perimeters. The number of churches increased to include a full range of denominations and the school popoulation was accommodated up to the 1970s in two infant schools, three junior schools and a comprehensive school on the edge of the town. The whole Mansfield/ Sutton/Kirkby area was producing evidence of high numbers of depressive illnesses, alcohol and drug abuse, non accidental injuries to young children, violence and criminal activities. The area is very close to Nottingham City which was leading the national statistics in crime behind London and Liverpool. By the 1970s the local colliery and the railway had long disappeared. Men were travelling to other collieries in nearby villages.

There was a thriving social life offered in the Miners Welfare Institutes, small drinking clubs and Bingo Hall. The Churches also provided the traditional range of Mothers Union and Young Wives Clubs. There was no theatre, cinema or swimming pool and few adult education courses locally.

There was a wide extended family network with a significant detail. Many of the women had had their children at a very young age. Thus some grandparents were young. Many such families also had five or six children. For women there was a pattern of factory employment, early marriage and pregnancies, twilight shifts or home work during their children's pre-school life and a return to full-time or day time work at statutory schooling age. Many husbands were on shift work at the factory and the pit. There was also a high rate of low income related poverty and unemployment.

Related Agencies

During the development of the nursery centre a new primary school and special school for ESN (S) & (M) was built on the same campus as the nursery with living accommodation for handicapped weekly boarders. Several nursery units were built in the nearby hamlets and a new comprehensive school was built in the centre of the town with some joint community and youth service use. A local community hall built in the 1950s was refurbished and offered a range of sport and recreational activities. It is important to note that the town had had few amenities prior to the 1970s. It then began to move gradually into a more encouraging situation of new educational opportunities and new health facilities.

Health visitors during the 1970s were adjusting to their 'reorganisation'. Their 'patch' schemes had changed to G.P. attachments. Many Health Visitors were concerned with changing their knowledge from a close involvement with a specific community to a diffuse approach and a need to liaise with other colleagues to meet the changing needs of the families. Instead of one health visitor being attached to a school, all the visitors at the Health Centre needed to be drawn into the liaison network. Their attitudes to nurseries were still essentially that a nursery place was a place of safety with appropriate standards of hygiene and feeding routines. It was also a place to put children to relieve their mothers. Once the child had a place this often relieved the health visitor to concentrate on other families.

Social workers were also adapting to new routines and expectations in the recently established Social Services Department. The nursery was very much seen as a resource for social workers, to place children from homes with severe problems into a place of safety. There was very little evidence in the early 1970s of nursery staff contributing to preventative social work by working closely with the families concerned. That was the social worker's job.

These attitudes and expectations needed to be explored by health visitors, social workers and the nursery staff if they were to effect a substantial change in the cycle of deprivation by involving parents in decision making and changing the custodial elements of day care. The exciting educational opportunities now available earlier to children could be significant in compensating for early educational disadvantage, but this could only be achieved by involving parents, and raising their expectations as important agents in their child's learning progress. The fact that the nursery was so closely linked to the education system introduced a new strand of opportunity for second chance and continuing education for the adults.

Working Relationships

These changes of direction and demands caused staff to reflect on their needs for further inservice training. They created the need for change in attitudes to existing work patterns, to working with parents and to accepting advice from other professionals. Many times in the early years one could hear the comment 'Well we can't do that can we?' challenged by the reply 'Well why not?' This gradually changed to staff saying 'Would it be possible or viable to . . . ?' 'I'd like to try this or that.' This was quite a significant change from the days when Headteachers and Matrons 'ruled', and staff got on with the job. The emphasis was now to work together as a team with everyone offering ideas, solutions or suggestions. The expectation of creative thinking, exploring ideas, adapting practice, abandoning the unworkable produced much conflict as staff had to develop discussion techniques, confidence to challenge or be challenged, trust and sympathy for each other and respect differences of opinion. There was a great change in practice from irregular staff meetings to an expectation of regular planning and consultation. Meetings now involved the teachers and nursery nurses and sometimes included cooks and cleaners as well as health visitors and social workers.

One aspect of the struggles in the early years was the lack of a blueprint or guidelines from the local authority. The Headteacher was given a great deal of responsibility, as in all schools. There was belief that the Head had the management skills to bring together a large staff, the organisational skills to meet the needs of large numbers of young children and the communication skills to liaise and co-operate with parents, other schools, governors, the social work department, health centres, probation office, training establishments, hospitals, voluntary agencies and the demands of administrators at local and county hall level. This aspect of state provision is quite fascinating. There are so many good points in favour of this apparent free rein to develop a school (or nursery) to meet the needs of a community. There are however some basic requirements in that staff need sensitive support from the advisory service as well as the local education and social service departments. Where there is change and innovation there is a need for elementary human support to encourage and praise effort, acknowledge difficulties and relieve anxieties.

Administrative barriers, departmental philosophies and local authority organisation produced a great number of problems which needed speedy resolutions to reduce stress for staff and in many cases for families. This new provision had a governing body constituted as a primary school. As with the local school it met three times a year. In the early stages of developing the centre it would have been very beneficial to have had more meetings particularly to tackle the bureaucratic problems which emerged frequently. Thus a close supportive network had to be developed by the senior staff with local colleagues in the department and in other agencies, and with staff struggling in other nursery centres. This meant someone regularly at the end of a phone or a friendly shoulder to lean or cry on.

Staff Strains

There was a great deal of staff change in the first two and a half years of the Centre's development. By the time I had arrived as Head of the Centre, there had been three different periods of Headship, a peripatetic head from the county education service covering for two spells of absence from the first Head. There has been two Matrons and two Deputy Heads. The Scale 1 class room teacher had changed as had many nursery nurses. There had been a dramatic rate of staff turnover. The National Children's Bureau research into the combined centres quite rightly relates some staff changes to dissatisfaction with the job and the new demands expected of them. However at Kirkby there was an interesting range of other factors. All the staff were women. Some very young and recently trained, some newly married, others hoping to start families. There were three 'women-centred' factors for staff change. One factor involved staff moving to another area with the husband's job. Another factor was a rapid number of pregnancies amongst the young teaching and nursery nurse staff. A third factor was staff moving to work in nursery classes as they were built in nearby towns providing staff with school hours and holidays in line with those of their own school age children. The first Matron took the opportunity to train as a teacher at the nearby Polytechnic. Within a year of my arrival I had appointed another Deputy Head and another Matron. It was inevitable that this period of instability affected staff development, and also affected attempts to develop a viable policy of flexibility and continuity and a limited development of liaison with voluntary and statutory agencies.

CHAPTER 3

Communications – a framework for development

Many staff involved with the early years now recognise the need for good communication skills. This chapter shares the learning experienced by staff with no formal training in these essential skills. It shows the intense interest generated by the regular flow of visitors all expecting clearcut aims and policies for development. It also reveals the conflict of traditional training towards changes in practice and philosophy. The mutual respect and delegation of responsibilities between the Head and the Matron are reflected in the team building, raising of awareness of each other's strengths and skills and development of support networks.

Working in a local authority establishment is rather like walking in the maze in a stately garden. There are a number of paths leading to closed walls, blind alleys and confusing directions, so there are moments of hope and excitement that the path is leading into the open, which can change into faltering steps bordering on despair that the end will never be in sight. The bureaucratic systems present the newly appointed Headteacher with hedges to be negotiated with care, taking tentative steps towards one area of support and information and sidestepping into others. Sometimes the steps or strides taken with enthusiasm and commitment are blocked by professional barriers, by power struggles within the administration at district and county level and by changes in political policies which do not match the needs of the community served.

The establishing of a new combined centre in an authority presents a newcomer with expectations of development. First one assumes that most of the staff are aware of the opportunity to try out new ideas and remove the constraints often experienced in the traditional nursery school or day nursery. Herein lay the first problem. Most nursery nurses and two of the nursery teachers had taken posts at the Centre because of the need for a job, any job, following their recent training. Several staff had recently trained in Derbyshire. There was very little provision in that county so they were prepared to travel into Nottinghamshire for work. Other staff lived in the town of Kirkby or very nearby and that provided limited financial outlay to get to work. For a large proportion of the young nursery nurses the far seeing options and planning of the senior management staff was quite divorced from their reality. Many were in their first jobs, and had begun firm relationships leading towards engagement and marriage. With the large turnover in staff in the first few years at the centre, they were confused, insecure and trying to do a good job with the children often under quite stressful relationships within their team and hierarchy of the Centre.

The second assumption that a new Head might make is that there would be a support system with regular management meetings to assess initiatives, identify administrative problems and work in a team with the Head and the staff to overcome initial problems and encourage progress made. The new Head would also expect regular visits of the Social Services and Education Advisors with responsibility for the under fives and a well established pattern with appropriate inservice training. As there were two combined centres within six miles of each other, there would be an expectation of close collaboration, exchange of ideas and problems shared too with local primary schools and special schools which would receive children from the centres at 5 years of age. But the reality was quite different and produced quite unnecessary stress on the senior staffs in both centres.

First, the centre had the traditional primary school governing body. This consisted of district and county councillors representing the two main political parties, a representative of the local education office, occasionally the Area Education Officer, but more often an administrative clerk with no particular interest, understanding or involvement in the centre's work, one parent and a member of staff. Both the Head and the Matron presented reports to this body. They met only three times a year and it became quickly evident how little influence the governing body had to deal with some early administrative problems, and how limited an interest or understanding a number of the members had in the centre. Within a year of working in the centre, the political climate had changed dramatically and the value and commitment to pre-school developments was seriously curtailed. Often the governors meetings were very strained as individual members repeatedly challenged the way we were working.

The National Childcare Campaign was firmly supported by many of the centre staff in that parents should be directly involved in planning and controlling the provision which is there to meet their needs. One parent representing nearly one hundred families is gross under-representation. No health visitor and no social worker input also seemed a vital loss to the future planning and development of centre strategies and policies.

Within a term of arriving at the Centre, the local Early Years Adviser retired. Within a year the Early Years Adviser in Mansfield, in another district, also moved to another post with another L.E.A. The vast expansion of part-time nursery education was supported by two Advisers, one a Senior Primary Adviser based at County Hall with wide ranging primary responsibilities and another based in Nottingham City. The support of local Headteachers was a link system with the Advisers at the local Area Office. There was a District Inspector who happened to be a Primary Inspector (in other districts he could have been a Secondary Adviser) and a team who had a number of schools usually based on a pyramid of feeder schools into a comprehensive school, with a pastoral responsibility. This meant a Maths Inspector with sound expertise in a basic curriculum subject and much secondary experience was allocated to the Nursery Centre. Although a great friend and very helpful, his annual visit was not really useful. The occasional visits of the Senior Adviser and a Social Services Adviser from County Hall were often pastoral rather than business like. Developments took place rapidly and problems resolved themselves slowly.

The communication between the Centre and the schools in the town was again of an incidental nature. Headteachers met once a term to discuss general district and county problems. It was impossible to develop these supposedly supportive meetings into a planned programme of educational experience for children from under 3 to

18 years with a corresponding development of community and continuing education for adults.

Other meetings of Headteachers were once or twice a year with the whole district attending to meet with the Director. These rarely offered opportunities for real discussion between the Headteachers.

Thus the first priority was to focus on the challenge of effective communication between the staff, between the parents and staff, between the Education Department and the Centre, and between the Social Services Department and the Centre. Very quickly this was extended to further communications with Health visitors, paediatricians, school nurse and doctor, N.S.P.C.C. inspectors, playgroups and childminders and a number of voluntary agencies.

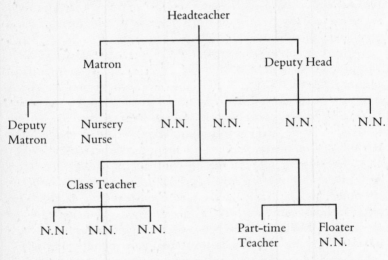

Figure 3.1   Fostering a team approach: The Staff

Fostering a team approach

In the early years there were many problems regarding the deployment and responsibility of the Head, Matron and Deputy Head. Having visited Centres where the recognition of a senior member of staff having overall responsibility for the establishment was not very common, we found it was crucial to the development of an integrated unit to accept that there was a Head with the ultimate responsibility to deploy specialist staff.

As children under three years of age are the responsibility of the Social Services Department, the Matron and her deputy had to ensure the highest standards of care of babies and toddlers. The referral of families by social workers, probation officers, health visitors and the National Society for the Prevention of Cruelty to Children to the Centre presented a new opportunity to support families with severe difficulties. Thus children were referred at a very early age for a range of physical, social, emotional or intellectual developmental reasons. The key family worker often grasped the fact that support to the parent, relative or other care person could offer preventative rather than compensatory and crisis measures in serious situations which may or may not focus on the child. The implications for the nursery staff were enormous if this preventative element was expressed in the expectations of working with very young children.

The first aim of the Baby Den (the under three unit) was to be positive, outward looking and family based, with a strong motivation to work as closely as possible with the families and their key workers. The staff were to work towards support and encouragement for families trying to develop their parenting skills, and avert family breakdown and intolerable stress.

The second important area of work was to offer a diagnostic assessment of children where key workers and families had already identified developmental delay, abnormality or handicap. Thus the traditional concept of 'looking after' children in the absence of their parents resulting in a rather custodial and passive outlook changed into a more radical concept that staff and parents work together, and that many admissions to the Baby Den would be part-time and supportive rather than full-time and custodial.

The third element of caring for young children in group situations acknowledges a demand by parents for day care places for their children whilst they are in full-time or part-time employment. But as the Centre had a limited number of places the admission of children of working parents was restricted to families with a variety of difficulties which employment could sometimes alleviate.

The Matron and her team were expected to work with families and other colleagues in the community if consistent assessment, counselling, reporting and exchange of skills and knowledge was to be achieved. This radical change in outlook required a perceptive Matron with a range of skills. The Matron had a professional responsibility to the Social Services Department and an administrative responsibility to report to the governing body and to attend case conferences. She also had a professional responsibility to work very closely with the Head of the Centre to develop the quality and consistency of care and learning opportunities throughout the long extended day and full year of fifty weeks opening.

Within six months of my arriving at the Centre the third Matron in 3½ years was appointed. It was an excellent appointment as she also had not arrived in her post through the conventional channels of promotion. Her experience and contribution to the playgroup movement was similar to the Head's and this had influenced her philosophy towards day care.

The first priority was to meet regularly, to inform each other honestly about concerns, to share ideas and plan together to establish a recognition in the staff that the Matron and Head liked each other, were working in partnership towards similar philosophies.

The Centre was over visited by a wide assortment of people in those early years! The National Children's Bureau research officers thankfully did not include our Centre in their research. If they had we were convinced that we would have contributed to the grim account of early progress in the new combined centres. Visitors included administrators, councillors, lecturers, teacher trainers, CQSW staff, advisors, Directors of Education and Social Services from other authorities and many, many students. Although this often placed more work on the Head and Matron and other staff we welcomed the interest because much of the close questioning clarified our ideas, our practice and our progress and often identified gaps or highlighted a new strategy to explore. Throughout this 'goldfish period' the Matron and the Head together talked with visitors. Where mistakes were made mutual counselling often presented new approaches. Where success was identified in any aspect of the Centre work, a shared cup of coffee and a brief feeling of 'getting there' was essential. It was important to grasp that the Centre was moving towards its potential as a family resource even though a new crisis might set us problems and often prevent us from acknowledging the ordinary good everyday things that happened.

Besides consultation and shared planning the Matron and the Head supervised the extended day and year on a shift system with staggered holidays to work towards this consistency of quality and standards. This shift system also provided the essential continuity for parents and other agencies.

The Deputy Matron had a role similar to the teaching staff. She lead a team of assistants and established the day-to-day routine of the Baby Den under the guidance of the Matron. She was the key member of staff with the under threes, as her shift where possible, was always the middle shift (traditional school hours) to enable her to work when most of the children were present, thus establishing daily contact with most parents. She had an important role in liaising with the teaching staff when children moved into the nursery family groups. In the absence of the Matron, due to shifts, holidays and meetings, the Deputy Matron also took administrative responsibility, attended case conferences and made decisions affecting the children, parents and staff. She also had to work very closely with the Head and Deputy Head to be aware of all aspects of development.

The Deputy Head was also a class teacher. She worked with her team of nursery assistants and the part-time teacher to promote the continuity of educational standards and counter-balance the effects of shifts, staggered holidays, part-time and full-time placements and other flexible arrangements. She had an important role in home-visiting, supporting parents and liaising with other professionals, not only those referring to the Centre, but the local primary schools and special schools in the community and specialists such as the speech therapist and psychologist. She had the final responsibility for decisions, usually in consultation with the Matron, during the absence of the Head.

This quartet of senior staff challenged the expectations of senior post holders in traditional nursery schools and day nurseries. The most important aspect of the work was to develop team work with excellent channels of communication. There was a respect for individual expertise and responsibilities, confirmed by a commitment to trusting, liaising, sharing and supporting each other. There was an essential need for flexibility, patience and delegation. There was an acceptance of overlapping skills combined with an acknowledgement of specialist expertise and experience.

By August 1977 there were eight other nursery nurses as new conditions of service were offered so that they could choose the Social Service longer hours with short holidays option or the Education Department's shorter working day with long holidays. Understandably most chose the Education conditions of service. As there was a significant loss of nursery nurse working hours, a new post was created. This new post holder was to work with the three teams and cover during holiday absences.

The staff working with the under threes were all qualified nursery nurses. With the older children the teams consisted of teaching staff who had experience in nursery and infant work with nursery assistants all with NNEB qualifications. Some nursery nurses had worked in day nurseries only during training. Many were in their first job.

What were the expectations of the staff when they first began to work at the Centre? How did they change? What were the greatest demands made on their experience and skills working in a Nursery Centre?

The staff were given a few questions to consider the learning experienced by the variety of women thrown together in this new establishment.

One might expect them to be fired with enthusiasm to pioneer a new educational venture. One might also expect them to view the Centre as a place to work which could offer new challenges and job satisfaction. Yet there was a whole spectrum of sensible but separate perceptions.

I expected to care for the children and the teachers to do the teaching.

I didn't know really what to expect. Having spent a year of my training in a nursery unit and then worked in a day nursery, many years ago, I couldn't possibly imagine how the two could combine.

I think I hoped I would be able to contribute to the character of the nursery and respond to the challenges of the then new idea of Social Services and Education joining together. I looked forward to working in a large group of staff. I really believed I would be working in a purpose built nursery.

I hoped I would have responsibility over a small group of children for whom I would care and form relationships, to help them in their individual development. I wanted to have experience working with and helping disadvantaged children.

I was told by the office, part-time mornings only, for one term. I think I thought of myself as an individual teacher at first, not so much a member of a team.

Initially I was a very young and inexperienced teacher straight from college. Like all newly qualified teachers I had to apply to a county for a post, not a specific job vacancy. Finishing college, I secured a supply post at the Centre until the end of the summer. In the autumn I was offered the full-time post. My first year was confusing with three different head-teachers. I do remember having to come to terms with shifts, the holiday system and the large number and variety of staff.

I don't think I anticipated the type of problems encountered leading a team.

Work, Overwork and Communications

During the early years we struggled with a range of communication patterns which tried to meet everybody's needs. The fullness of the day and so many children and families presented every member of staff with tiredness problems. Working with distressed families drained staff emotions and energy. Opportunities to sit and talk together were few. Staff arrived on different shifts between 8 a.m. and 10 a.m. and left between 3 p.m. and 6 p.m. Lunch supervision was staggered with no one having more than a half hour break and children were being supervised between 3.45 p.m. and 5.30 p.m. so that staff meetings could never have the full staff present. Staggered holidays added to the communication difficulties.

First it was essential for the four senior staff to meet each week formally to look back over the week and to plan for the next. Information on families, children, other agency involvement, staff and so on was shared. It was very necessary to have a clear understanding of proposed developments, case conferences and new colleagues to work in the community. It was also a useful time to 'let off steam' when patience and hurt and tiredness required sympathetic nurturing. The dynamics of this group was interesting. Differing members took the lead in being the sustainer or being sustained. The meeting was not always chaired or opened by the Head. There was time allocated for each of the four to talk on a subject of their choice, either a problem or a suggestion for further consideration. In these meetings we shared ideas about counselling staff, made painful decisions about families, about handling very disturbed children and about difficulties with our links with other agencies or our own departments.

These skills were often new to us. We had had no training for individual or group counselling. Our previous work experience had not prepared us for the severity of the family difficulties we were to share, or for the range of handicap and special educational needs we were to identify. These weekly meetings which provided a forum to seek help, delegate individual skills and keep up to date with the demands being made on the nursery staff as well as the individual senior staff.

Fostering the nursery staff communication network was a time-consuming necessity. Everyone was to be welcomed each day and an interest taken in them to raise their self image and esteem and pay tribute to their work. The cooks in the kitchen required time and interest. Complimenting meals, making new suggestions, expecting flexibility with numbers of meals and taking an interest in them as individuals as well as being concerned about their children, relatives and holidays. The cleaners and the laundress were equal concerns for attention and praise. The casual daily enquiry and contact was reinforced with an occasional tea party in the office, and sharing in all staff and nursery functions. The valued expertise of the clerical assistant was also nurtured as her job changed significantly with the development of curricular and philosophy documents, newsletters and increased report writing.

As staff arrived there was a quick verbal account of something which might affect a child or a parent. A staff noticeboard publicised meetings, courses and various social activities. Each Monday the three teams were given a Staff Bulletin which listed the anticipated activities.

For example:

Monday	Jenny on leave Activity 1
	Jill with her family Group
	S.W. visiting Baby Den about . . . .
	H. V. Student to spend day in Activity 11
	Julia at Heads Meeting in Sutton p.m.
	Ann on course at Basford Hall p.m.
Tuesday	Case conference for . . . . . .
	Visitors from Humberside County Council
	Nursery nurse tutor to visit Mary in Baby Den
	Parent Toddler Group and Toy Library p.m.
	Act 1 Team Meeting

Wednesday	Visitors from Derby Lonsdale College
	Coreen at meeting at Health Centre
	Margaret take Family Group out in mini bus
	Gingerbread in Parents Room p.m.
	Act 11 Team Meeting
Thursday	Parent Toddler Group and Toy Library a.m.
	Baby Den Team Meeting at lunch time
	W.E.A. Women and Health Group p.m.
	Staff Meeting
Friday	Children's day Support Group a.m.
	Coffee afternoon for new parents

This bulletin helped to prepare staff or remind them of absences and visitors as well as some of the group community activities going on in the Parents' room.

Staff and Team Meetings

This was one of the most problematic areas for dispute, anxiety, resentment and even hostility. Interestingly all the teaching staff expected regular staff meetings and felt the need for them. It was a very challenging job to help many of the nursery nurses understand the need for them and their role in the group, to help them develop more confidence and skills in a group debate, and to be convinced that the meetings were attempting to be democratic and power sharing.

Establishing a pattern of regular planning and consultation meetings was exhausting and often very unsatisfactory. We had to accept that rarely would we ever have all the staff at a meeting together. We tried various strategies – monthly meetings, fortnightly meetings, tea with children playing at our feet whilst we talked and were interrupted by a collecting parent, planned agendas, free agendas, differing chairperson, and staff meeting minutes for absent colleagues. In reality the organisation and the timing of the meetings was relatively unimportant compared with the attitudes of a proportion of staff that the meetings had little value for them. We stumbled on with differing approaches for instance –

(A) One team would prepare a short account of something they had successfully worked through and share it with the rest of the staff. Then came the business section of notices and information. This might be followed by discussing a new idea or process which could be presented by anyone, but in the early days was more usually introduced by a senior staff or a teacher.

(B) The meeting would focus on equipment. A particular activity in the nursery programme would be selected, perhaps sorting objects. Everyone was requested to provide a box of improvised sorting materials instead of using the commercial equipment in the nursery. This produced some very good discussions and helped lead to more planned preparation for learning activities and away from a reliance on random selection of existing equipment.

(C) Working party feedbacks. Staff would volunteer to meet in small groups to consider an aspect of Centre work and prepare a discussion document or diagram for a staff meeting. These were successful in involving most staff in the small groups but inevitably a teacher or senior staff member reported back and led the discussion at full staff meetings.

Everyone was invited to participate in the process of developing the Centre. Many staff responded and grew in confidence within their team and within the general work of the Centre. The Head and Matron would have benefitted from a management course at this time to help them understand the group process and have clearer objectives matched to their style of leadership. We had to come to terms with the range of personality traits from cook through to Head. We had to accept the opposites and work out ways of complementing staff idiosyncracies.

Cartwright and Zander's work gave us some insight into Group Dynamics. We identified our own staff's personality traits and acknowledged some with an extended approach and commitment to their work. We understood some of the restricted outlooks of other staff and tried to approach some of these restricted attitudes, through counselling, personal contact and praise and encouragement. Many expected the Head or Matron to dictate policies or tasks. Some were insecure with the expectation of consultation and decision making. Their dependence on leadership led to many meetings where staff felt insecure in understanding the new rules and tasks. The initial emotional resistance to the new demands was extended by the frequent turnover of staff resulting in a renewed approach to accommodate new members to the team. However the smaller team meetings, which did meet on a weekly basis, provided the opportunity for mutual support to flourish, an open exchange of views to be expressed and a feeling of co-operation to develop. As relationships improved throughout the Centre, roles were established and developed and more energy was available to channel into effective work. There was always a balancing act. The senior management skills were developing one step ahead of the staff or emerging through practice, intuition, common sense and intense analysis after the staff meetings. We either sat in glum, drained silence after the staff had left feeling totally inadequate in the democratic procedures, or we smiled with a feeling of wonder that the meeting had felt right, that a certain member of staff had contributed with enthusiasm, and that the outcome of the meeting was positive and successful. Occasionally we shed a tear whilst we washed up the tea things and wondered if it would be better to return to the authoritarian style and just announce the new tasks and expect people to get on with it.

Very few staff felt that they did not have to make some adjustments to accommodate their position in the Centre team. Some staff contributed enormously to the Centre's increasing aspiration to act as a resource for families in the community. What were the most challenging demands on their experience and skills?

If I am honest, it's not the children or the parents but the staff that have made the most demands; such as supporting another member of staff through a long illness of depressions and personal problems, trying to implement the high standards set by the senior staff, not having confidence to express myself therefore needing to use all my skills to do the job within the boundaries set. Let's face it the job is one long challenge.

Dealing with the other adults in the team. Coming to terms with my own limitations and those of others where they affected our work.

I was a young and inexperienced teacher. I now feel I have achieved a great sense of personal development. I have become a more caring, loving teacher, aware of not only the children's needs and development and the needs of their families, but also aware of the staffs.

You cannot be a typical classroom teacher. You have to be prepared to work with other people in a team. You have to adjust to the amount of responsibility given to direct work or an activity within the Centre. Another difference is the amount of freedom for individuals to use their initiative.

CHAPTER 4

First impressions: crises, stresses and small successes

Co-operation and liaison are the vital concern not only of practition-
ers in the voluntary, local authority and local health services for young
children, but equally of those who provide and manage services.

DHSS/DES Circular
LASSL/78/1

This chapter is an account of the crises and stresses of combined
centres as they develop. The earlier theme of contradictory criteria
for admissions is developed and clarifies the conflict between Social
Services and Education philosophies. It continues with the first hand
experience of meaningful parent and child contact exposing the
stress for staff particularly with overcrowding and confrontations.
However there were rewards and small successes and signs that the
Centre was beginning to meet the needs of the community.

Admissions Criteria

The community of Kirkby produced as many varied challenges for
key workers and nursery staff as any inner city area could have
offered. Our great strength was probably ignorance! We tried to
respond to a kaleidoscope of demands from agency colleagues and
the parents at the same time as trying to establish our roles, goals and
networks. We had reservations about our abilities and we usually

accepted the new experiences working them out as we went along. It was reassuring to have tremendous support from the senior social workers and we gradually developed the most trusting partnership with health colleagues in the clinic and the paediatric assessment unit.

First we had to overcome some of the bureaucratic barriers which confused parents, certainly confused the nursery staff and consistently resulted in problems being pushed between departments as 'the other's problem'. The nursery centre was expected to offer support and guidance for parents, wider learning and social experience for the children and social and recreational opportunities for the family. The previous division between care and education had been the root cause of a great many conflicts and discrepancies. A fundamental change should have been the positive reorganisation of admission criteria and fees. But still the two departments which funded the Centre had quite different criteria and two opposing policies for admission.

Social Services criteria for admission were selective and socially divisive as places for day care were so scarce. All families had to establish evidence of severe need. This could include single parents who needed to work, maternal illness, maternal incapacity, mental disorders, distress and depression, children with behaviour problems likely to threaten family unity, child abuse and handicap. The fee structure was relatively simple. Parents with children under three years were charged 60 pence a day regardless of the time spent at the Centre, i.e. for one hour or 10 hours with three meals. Social Workers could offer a nil assessment in certain cases. All children from a few months to 5 years were eligible for fees during the school holidays.

The Education Department criteria for admission were seemingly open ended. A place was available for all families who required one and it was free. There was a charge of 50 pence for lunch (as in all schools) but with a free meal scheme related to families receiving Supplementary Benefits and Family Income Supplements. However such a place and provisions were not available to children under the age of 3 years.

The most difficult administrative procedure however related to the fact that the Education Department operated during school term time. The Social Services Department had responsibility for children under 3 during the term time only and for children aged 0–5 during the holidays. This meant that children entitled to a free place in term time paid 60 pence in the holidays, even though they were the children often with the most difficulties and risks.

Here are some examples of typical administrative problems which could have been averted with a simpler policy.

M. aged 2 years 10 months admitted on Social Services criteria; severe marital stress, violence, inadequate mothering skills, poor childcare. Fee 60 pence a day. Father employed. M. aged 3 years is transferred to Education register and a free place with lunch at 50 pence. During the holiday the fee returns to 60 pence.

C. is 2 years 6 months. Mother is single parent with two children. Mother is very ill and C. admitted full-time. Fee 60 pence. Mother on Supplementary Benefit and irregular with paying fees. C. is 3 and transfers to the Education register. She has a free place and automatic assessment for free lunch as mother is on Supplementary Benefit. During the holiday the place is now free in line with the free school meal.

J. is 4 years old. Mother is single, close to violent anger and loss of control. Support for J. to attend several afternoons each week to relieve tension, support depressed mother and help active, boisterous child. J's place is free during term time but he must pay 60 pence during the holiday even though he does not have a meal.

V. and S. were admitted following their parents divorce and mother became employed and also received Family Income Supplement. V. is 2 years and required to pay the 60 pence fee but S. is 3 years old and has a free place with a free meal. In the holiday S. still has a free place even though she is three but V. pays the 60 pence. V. has her third birthday and automatically has a free place too.

There were hundreds of arrangements like these which were complex administratively and exasperating to families and senior staff who had to find their way around the bureaucratic muddle. What was sad was that the administrators did not view the system as a muddle of conflicting criteria but as a clear concise procedure applicable to two different types of establishment.

Family situations change, sometimes gradually with little disturbance or trauma, sometimes dramatically with violence, loss of parent, employment or accommodation. Difficulties in marital relationships can be resolved amicably or with great bitterness. Poor housing and unemployment can lower adult morale and self esteem and produce apparently uncaring, apathetic and dirty families. Children exposed to consistent violence, unstable parenting and regular disturbance, can adapt to their experiences by withdrawal of co-operation, affection and communication or by destructive disturbed behaviour or assumed normal behaviour concealing the effects of dissension and confusion. Men and women hurt by poor marital experiences, struggling with low paid jobs and inferior housing with large families often require support to rebuild their confidence and stability to face the future, make decisions and enjoy their family. Working with very young children presents difficulties in separating the parents' needs from those of the children. They are so interwoven, so interdependent that nursery staff require new skills to counsel families wisely and sympathetically; to plan together for the children's needs and to work towards a close, caring and sharing relationship.

It is essential to have an open mind regarding family need. One cannot have a rigid list of criteria because each family's needs are individual. One can accept the limitations of the resource to meet the need, but staff must take care not to impose moralistic attitudes to family situations which are unusual, different or seemingly hopeless. It is therefore important that staff expertise and understanding be extended so that they can accept families at the stage they are at, and work towards developing a trusting relationship.

It is true to say that none of the teaching staff had been involved in the type of family crises regularly handled by social workers. Few of the nursery nurses had had comparable experiences as so many of them had been so recently trained. The challenge was in establishing patterns of involvement with the other agencies and the families themselves to prevent family breakdown, support family crises and provide quality day care and educational experiences for the children and it was sometimes overwhelming.

During the first few years the demand made on the staff at the Centre were extraordinary.

First Contact Experiences

Traditional day care had for many years been used as a place of safety for children whilst the key social worker helped families in severe difficulties outside the establishment. The change in approach in the Social Services towards preventative work and intervention and support before 'crisis level' had to be responded to in the Centre. We tried to involve parents and their key worker from Social Services, the hospital, or the clinic in decisions around admission options and policies. For example, the key worker was expected to bring the parent(s) to the Centre with their child(ren) supported if necessary by other members of the family to discuss the arrangements we would offer. We felt strongly that parents should be informed of the options for the child's admission and the expectations of the staff for close involvement with the family.

This first contact was to include consultation and assessment, sharing each other's knowledge of the child(ren), reviewing arrangements together and understanding the partnership in the contract between the family, the key worker in the other agency and the Centre staff. This was time consuming. It meant social workers and health visitors could not ring up and put clients names down on 'priority' waiting lists. It meant parents were accompanied by a known person for their first entrance into the Centre. For many parents the initial welcome to the Centre to discuss their needs was confusing. There were serious problems perhaps non-accidental injury proceedings, homelessness, handicap or involvement with the prison service, and many just expected to be told what they could have in terms of number of sessions, fees to pay and hours of opening. Instead they found a quiet room with a cup of coffee, some easy chairs and some sympathetic people who wanted to offer the most useful and helpful arrangements to suit their child and themselves.

For example, many expected their child 'to be taken' from them and admitted to the Centre for 50 weeks of the year, with little access to them during the day. We tried to establish priorities with the family and their key worker. This might mean a five day place for a few weeks or months to enable the parent to be relieved of the pressures of the child's behaviour or handicap. There would be discussions of different involvements in the Centre to help the parent learn to cope with the child, improve their parenting skills, meet other parents, perhaps observe another professional working with the child. Several situations involved the physiotherapist, the speech therapist, the teacher of the deaf and the educational psychologist with the parent and the Centre staff to devise individual programmes for children. It was essential for parents with difficulties to understand the options and the possibility of changing them, and to be involved in the decision making process.

Our aim for children admitted for five full days throughout the year on 'crisis criteria' was to work with the family and key worker to lessen the crisis so that the child would again enjoy a regular homelife as well as the exciting play experiences a good nursery could offer. For families who worked and required the full day care option time was spent helping them appreciate our concern and commitment to talk regularly and share their child's progress. For many single parents coping with grief, anger, humiliation and guilt, the stress of working all day and collecting tired, fractious children and then continuing their day with housework and childcare was often too much. We tried to make the start and end of their child's day at the Centre as calm and loving as possible.

Daily Difficulties

However the tremendous range of family support took their toll on staff patience, endurance and emotional stability. We coped without appropriate training, experience and knowledge, with non-accidental injury; access to children under Centre supervision; community service orders on parents or cohabitees to work with us to develop parenting skills; with parents suffering from physical and mental ill health including depressive illnesses, schizophrenia, advanced multiple sclerosis and suicidal tendencies. We also encountered wife battering, sexual violence, rejection, poor child/parent bonding, severely emotionally disturbed young children and delayed development. Adjustment to involvement with this severity of social problems on the one hand and integrating families and their children who enjoyed fairly calm, happy and coping lives was a delicate balancing act.

Sometimes the Centre was charged with anger, violence and fear. Parents would enter a nursery room shouting, screaming abuse, throwing clothes, the child or any handy object. Staff would recoil in fear, confusion and distress. The senior staff had to be effective in diffusing quickly violent situations where children were upset, other parents and the staff subdued and anxious and the angry parent in a state which could change to tears and breakdown or physical violence. We had to establish our own understanding of the changing attitudes and skill required to cope in a calm, balanced and effective way.

There were a number of parents who could reduce the calm welcome of the Centre into this state of confusion. Staff needed much counselling and guidance as well as the physical presence of the senior staff to deflect these scenes. Miraculously no one was ever physically attacked by a parent, although on several occasions the situation was grave. We usually reacted by speaking quietly but very firmly and insisting that the parent withdrew from the crowded playrooms into the sanctuary of the office or staffroom or even the laundry room. With shaking knees and racing pulses we had to learn by experience how to deal with these outbreaks of hate, anger and guilt.

A Crowded Centre

Crises in the Centre combined with children's developmental needs required new approaches to staff discussion and consultation. New training events were provided by the two local authority departments and intensive support from the advisory staff. As we lurched from crisis to crisis it became obvious that our networks and professional development had to be generated by ourselves and we had to seek alternative forms of guidance. We relied heavily on social work support. We approached the Marriage Guidance Council for training sessions on counselling. We devised our own inservice events and coopted the help of the local Teacher Centre Warden in funding them. We developed regular visits to other establishments to collect ideas. There were visits to day nurseries, special schools, playgroups and hospitals. We helped establish the Nursery Centres Association, a national body, to provide a forum for support and progress. Our governing body fought a long and hard battle with both Education and Social Services to create opportunities for nursery nurses to join the region's Certificate in Social Services Course at Derby. This was the only further professional course available to them. After several years' debate, the Matron was accepted on the course, although the many criteria for acceptance were not fulfilled at first by the authority to ensure a smooth transfer on to the course and the smooth continuity of life in the Centre.

Whilst staff were struggling to establish their roles and practice,

ideas to enrich and support family life in the community began to
emerge. At one time 58 of our 96 children on role were not living
with both natural parents. There was much evidence of the need for
comfort and advice for the single parent.

The nearest Gingerbread groups were in Mansfield and Notting-
gham. As fares were so expensive it became necessary to investigate
the possibility of setting up a local group. Our tiny Parents' Room
was offered as a base for weekly meetings. This quickly increased to
add a monthly meeting during the week with a creche. Many parents
on the long waiting list for nursery places were desperate for help.
We offered a small playcourt, the indoor area for energetic boisterous activities, two sessions each week to establish a Mother/Toddler
Group. From this emerged the Toy Library. Social Services were
concerned that the town had no registered Childminder. A month's
campaign based partly at the Centre produced the nucleus of a later
thriving Childminders' Group. Our playcourt was made available
once a fortnight for their support group. Very quickly the Parents'
Room became an active group room which included toddlers and
babies accompanying their mother on her social outing. These children began wandering through the Centre unattended.

Understandably the staff began to find that opening up the Centre
to other users produced much more work, some stress and certainly
tensions between the senior staff and some of the parents who did not
'look after their kids'. In staff meetings, we had all felt that this community development was a positive way forward. There were no
extra staff provided to foster the work, supervise the parents or make
sure the children were appropriately cared for. We believed that the
parents should be self-regulating and organise themselves and take
responsibility. However the Centre was very small and cramped.
With fifteen staff and 60 children each day, the addition of an extra 20
toddlers and their parents on several days combined with the regular
loss of use of the playcourt for active play on wet, foggy days, it was
inevitable that tensions rose and tempers frayed.

The staff felt very strongly that we should be in control and that
the senior staff should be more realistic when encouraging the new
developments of parents meetings and workshops. The Centre was
built for the nursery children. It was not staffed to monitor and control its progress in these areas. On some days, particularly the long,
wet dark days of winter, (and in Kirkby they seemed to run into
weeks without any sign of the sun) the Centre was bursting at the

seams. Every area contained children and adults. The two playrooms and the four quiet dens were in constant use. The parents' area and the playcourt overflowed with babies, toddlers and laughing loud voiced women. Cigarette smoke filtered into the office, library and playcourt from the parents' area. Crisps and biscuits were ground into the carpet, ashtrays overflowed. The Head and Matron searched in vain for a quiet undisturbed corner to welcome a visitor, a new parent, another colleague.

On some days it was a madhouse, which left staff wrung out, exhausted, speechless and incapable of contributing calmly at a staff meeting, or a team planning group. On many evenings some staff fled from the Centre to the reality of their home, unable or unwilling to stay for a while to talk through the problems of the day. This meant that the four senior staff and often the two teachers relied on each other regularly to talk through the progress, problems and strategies.

Stresses upon staff

The main theme of this chapter has been to give a glimpse of the stresses which emerged at rapid speed whilst the staff were still learning to work together towards some common goals. It is impossible to describe the tiredness of working in this type of centre. The fact that it was open such long hours gave many opportunities for exploiting staff goodwill and commitment. Working shifts is emotionally traumatic at times. You begin at 8 a.m. and finish at 3 p.m. yet your team may be shortstaffed and need at least another ½ hour of your time. A child or parent in your family group may require more attention just as your shift finishes. Do you leave and hand them over to others or do you stay perhaps for another hour to sort it out? The staff or team meeting begin at 4 p.m. after most children have gone home. Your shift finishes at 3 p.m. There's no point in going home and returning. The meeting will not finish until 5.30 p.m. or 6 p.m. You will have committed yourself to 3 extra hours, having started work with children at 8 o'clock in the morning.

The paltry salary young nursery nurses receive does not take into consideration professional commitment outside the stated hours of work. We expected and received high standards of commitment. Yet there were times when young staff and even their new husbands needed some counselling from the Head or Matron about the need for time after the Centre closed to meet and talk, plan and evaluate, praise and encourage. The guilt for senior staff and the teachers of their higher salaries matching this out-of-hours commitment naturally gave rise to tension and conflict. Often these staff gave even more of their personal and family time to the Centre. All staff were expected to attend team and staff meetings unless they were on holiday and it was established that individuals should offer support to out-of-Centre activities on Saturdays and during the evenings when and if they could. But no one was to feel guilt about other commitments. Inevitably a small number emerged who supported most extra activities. We worked hard to help the team recognise other members family commitments, personal wishes and individual approach to the job.

There were examples of not coping with the pace of Centre life. Several staff left because they could not give what was expected. Two staff's health suffered badly as their own family life did not cushion or relieve the stress of work. One example remained stamped on the staff's memory. A very mature and respected nursery nurse flourished with the challenges and responsibilities. Her major work experience had been as a classroom assistant to an infant department in a primary school. She was redeployed to the Centre at a time of cutbacks and redundancies in nursery nurse jobs. Her personal strengths gave her a sound foundation to fit into the Centre team and make significant contributions to its development. She began attending courses, enjoyed her outside visits, attended her first residential conference. Her work with the children and her care for and interest in their families inspired many young and less experienced staff. Her relationship with the young teacher in her team mirrored her relationships throughout the Centre. Yet as she began to grow as an individual as well as a member of the team, there were conflicts in the family situation. She was not always at home with supper ready. Her evening activities included outings in a supportive women's group. Her family were expected to adapt to changes in the mother and the wife. This was a very human and tragic problem, which many women have to face. When the close family stability is threatened by new pressures and new developments, a choice has to be made. If your health is also suffering with the anxieties and tensions of work and home, inevitably a compromise has to be devised.

When this member of staff gave in her notice the Head and matron supported her wholeheartedly in the choice made. As she left the Head and Matron remained to wash up the pots in the staff room. One quietly sobbed into the washing up soapsuds, the other snivelled into the washing up cloth. We recognised ourselves and our families having to adapt and accommodate the changes in our lives and their lives with our involvement in the Centre. We felt utter failures that we had not cushioned our colleagues more, counselled and guided her and helped her family. It was a black spot in our progress. It unsettled our confidence that what was expected of staff was realistic and attainable. It was a time when we desperately needed advice, comfort and a little nurturing. Unexpectedly a local social worker arrived with a problem. She recognised our need and shelved her problem and got in touch with the senior social worker. Our discussions with him later that week helped put the failure into perspective and strengthened us and guided us in devising a new pattern of staff supervision.

Small Successes

During this time there was a spate of conferences and DES/DHSS circulars recommending low cost school provision. We had to justify the cost of fifteen staff working with 60 children. Our approach was to provide evidence that we needed more staff.

Our arguments included:–

(a) The decrease in family breakdown. Our social work and health colleagues became aware of a drop in the number of families with severe crises being referred to the Centre. Many were being identified 'at risk' and were introduced to the supportive regime at the earliest possible stage. This might begin with joining the Toy Library and Toddler group or attending the Gingerbread group. It might be an introductory visit on release from hospital with a young baby.

(b) The decrease in number of children going into care. The high staff ratio was giving more intensive help and guidance to families who benefitted from attendance at the Centre. One important post which has never been created was for a play therapist/family worker who could work on a one-to-one basis in the home as well as the Centre.

(c) The early identification of handicap, and special educational need. So many children were referred with developmental problems, some worrying but unidentified, others gross requiring a high staff/child ratio to ensure the daily structured programmes were completed for each child.

(d) The contribution to educational disadvantage – through working closely with the family combined with the teaching skills to prepare children to cope with the routines of statutory schooling and take their place with confidence and enthusiasm.

(e) The contribution to the quality of family life. We tried to offer and share our skills and knowledge of young children's development to help parents enjoy their children more by playing with them and understanding their needs. Opportunities to enjoy the support network with other parents combined with continuing workshops, courses and outings presented many parents with a changing view of new personal challenges and interests.

(f) Because the Centre was open 50 weeks of the year from 8–6 p.m. the staff were available to the community for all sorts of help and advice. Social workers and health visitors offices do not open until 9 a.m. and close at 5 p.m.–5.30 p.m. even 4.30 p.m. on Fridays. We often picked up all kinds of problems at each end of the day and contained or cushioned them until other help was available. Often our availability solved the problem. The high staff ratio was essential for integrating the work with the children, with the parents and with the community.

Alongside this progress in establishing quality day care, interest and partnership with families and other colleagues and a community education policy, the Centre staff considered many approaches to more effective learning for the young child. This included the early learning of the baby and toddler in an institution as well as appropriate routines to meet the needs of the part-time or full-time child, with minor or gross learning difficulties, and also others enjoying satisfactory health and social contact, eager and curious to explore their world around them.

CHAPTER 5

Building blocks – creating the right environment and relationships

Although the building was purpose built the staff struggled to make it less like an institution and more like home. Equipment and furniture was moved frequently as if changing the sets for its noisier and quieter periods. The staff are a feature in this environment too. Their appearance can be just as inappropriate and intimidating. In settling into a new building, we experimented with spaces such as Family Group Areas, Baby Den and Playcourt. These areas create fresh challenges for staff and particularly for the relationships between staff. This chapter concludes with staff responses to the effects of the environment on their roles.

Whilst institutional care for babies and toddlers is inappropriate, imaginative building design, high quality staff, and generous staff–child ratios can enhance the experience of young children who spend long days in group care situations. Children benefit and good staff relations and staff–parent relations can be fostered more easily.

If we consider the entitlement of all children attending a centre to include a comfortable, homelike environment we should try to provide a variety of room size and designated use, easy access to health and hygiene facilities, outdoor environments and furniture and fittings which blend the best aspects of home and institution.

In a specially designed unit restricted by economic considerations rather than planned around the child's needs, we invariably find the design of the building holds unnecessarily stressful areas, and accommodation with limited uses.

During a long day at the Centre some children need to rest or sleep for several hours, at any time of the day. Three meals may be required. Enormous demands are made on staff and the building in establishing individual patterns of care such as feeding, toileting and sleeping if children are not to be moulded into conformity to assist a smooth running for the convenience of staff. Let us consider the demands made on a building and its staff to meet the challenge of personalised day care and early educational experiences.

Imagine that young children eat, sleep, play and rest in completely open plan rooms with frequent changes of use organised around their large numbers. For example, thirty children may be in a classroom at the end of a morning session. Arrangements have to be made to clear away play activities, many of which are very messy, set out lunch tables attractively, complete chores such as cleaning materials and equipment, and look after children, all in the same area. Half the children will be collected by parents and taken home, the other half will need to wash and prepare for lunch. Lunch will be served in the same room as children being collected for lunch at home. At the end of the meal some children will need to sleep in a pram outside or in a cot or bed indoors. Others will need quiet restful indoor activities, more active and boisterous children will want outdoor play. Meal tables must be cleared, floors swept and washed and the afternoon activities set out in preparation for the part-time afternoon children arriving in threequarters of an hour's time.

When arranging rooms it is necessary to take into account what will appeal to parents too! Every room should have an idea for parents to feel comfortable to sit and observe and enjoy some refreshment without feeling they are getting in the staff or children's way. If there is an acceptance that staff and parents work closely together then the accommodation must show visible evidence of welcome, with armchairs, books and noticeboard. There must also be private accommodation for comforting and counselling parents in distress.

As the Centre offers part-time and full-time places throughout the day and indeed the year, the education facilities are an integral part of the care facilities. The rooms have multi-purpose use which means that staff must work as a team to consider and plan for the children's needs throughout the day.

Kirkby Centre's Environment

The Centre was originally designed to accommodate eighty children, half of whom would attend an extended day with a proportion requiring holiday placements. In the very early days it was obvious that the Centre could not admit such large numbers of children particularly as twenty of the children would be under three years of age. The Department of Education and Science Department of Health and Social Security then recommended that the Centre should accommodate a maximum of sixty, fifteen of whom would be under three.

Accommodation was so limited that every available space was used to provide areas where it would be possible for *small* groups of children to be cared for during the excessively stressful mid-day reorganisation. Thus the office, staff room, library, playcourt and outdoors may be in use as well as the designated but inadequate quiet dens.

Another important aspect in establishing the quality of living in an institution must be the comfort and attractiveness of the environment. Our Centre was the second built in the County. The financial cuts were already beginning to take effect. The CLASP Building is consortium's basic design grey inside with large areas of plate glass. Grey plastic covered fire walls, grey marley tiled floors, grey formica tables and work surfaces, and grey polypropylene chairs offering a real challenge to staff ingenuity to brighten the working and living areas.

The staff spent a great deal of time improving the physical environment for the children. Some walls were then given pretty washable wallpapers. Velvet and bright cotton cushions are scattered in book corners. Second hand armchairs take preference over the uncomfortable plastic covered upright benches fixed to the wall. Plants, indoors and out, trees and flowering shrubs, improve the colour and textures around and give the children an awareness and appreciation of the world about them. These are all basic elements of life essential in a quality of experience denied many residents in run down industrial areas. Trying to create quiet areas for relaxation, rest and reading in a noisy, open-plan building is a challenge, particularly if there is to be easy movement of children in large numbers.

An outline of a 'typical' busy day gives an insight into the family atmosphere developed at the Centre.

A Typical Day

The early shift provides a wonderful start to the day. Staff arrive and chat to the cook and cleaner, before beginning to set the nursery room out with equipment. Parents begin to arrive with children for breakfast. This is a valuable time for a few shared moments: to exchange pleasantries, news of a family event, a problem with a child, some encouragements, or a joke or two. The young child sees the parent and staff as friends and moves from one relationship to the new one with a kiss and wave at the window as parent walks away down the path. The child might help setting out activities, or choose a toy or book and sit quietly until breakfast. In some cases an event at home the night before or just before leaving for nursery might have upset the child. A parent might still be angry or worried and this sometimes is reflected in the child who might need more help and comfort at the parting time. A parent who has overslept will arrive in a rush and the child might need a gentle wash and hairbrush to settle him in after the run to the nursery. Whatever the situation, time is given to the child/parent separation.

Cook will indicate that breakfast is nearly ready. Children enjoy laying the table cloth, setting out places, smelling the flowers and selecting their chair. A 'family' meal then takes place encouraging social skills and conversation. Utensils, plates and cups are stacked and cleaned; independence in helping themselves to milk, marmalade etc. is encouraged, time is given to the slow eater, conversation is enjoyed throughout the meal. It is a delightful time. There have, however, been some of the most disturbed children attending breakfast. The tensions at meal time then require very patient handling. This provides opportunities to share experiences and handling techniques between the parent and the staff. During these difficult periods staff are grateful for a weekly shift system as early morning tensions do not suit everyone. Time is given to help these children understand the patterns of socially acceptable behaviour. It is an interesting part of our students' training as many aspects of child development and family dynamics are discussed.

At the end of breakfast the other children begin to arrive. Some will come for the morning, others will stay for lunch, and a few will stay until 3.30 p.m. More staff arrive on the middle shift. Parents are greeted and a great deal of time is spent in relating to families and settling children down. Parents will be in every area in the Centre at this time. Prams and buggies choke the entrance. Babies and toddlers join in some play or scream in anger at having to leave the older sibling at nursery. Parents can be found chatting in the cloakroom and quiet dens, playing at an activity table, reading a book in the book corner, making tea in the parents room, having an earnest talk or a helpless weep in the office.

Staff focus on making this time of day important in bridging the gap from home into nursery. They concentrate on noting parents as people, not just Jane's mummy or Tony's grandma. Compliments to changing hairstyles, new false teeth, a new dress are exchanged. Parents with enormous problems are reassured or listened to, perhaps taken into a quiet corner for a more private chat. Some parents will sit in the nursery, silent, mute with depression. A cuddle, a smile, a cuppa is on hand. Parents who are aggressive and demanding are welcomed in varying ways, the senior staff ensuring that they are around to deal with a crisis or to give the parent the needed attention that an unsure and timid nursery staff could not. This is a vital support for staff. They need reassurance that it is not a failure to fear a powerful, aggressive parent. These parents need a strong, caring staff member to help them as much as the depressed and inadequate parents.

It is such a busy hour. People coming and going, the many contrasts of quiet, absorbed play and boisterous active movement with loud raucous adult laughter and mute unsmiling anxiety. Staff have to turn to each contrast and adjust their skills and behaviour accordingly. By about 10 o'clock many parents have left to go home, go shopping, go to work, join the toddler group, or take their place in the parents' room. Some remain as rota helpers to work alongside staff, others remain quietly in an armchair for companionship or comfort rather than return home and take an overdose or sit in isolation.

At lunch time and tea time a similar pattern emerges. Families returning to collect children before lunch or after the meal have access to individual staff. They arrive early and observe the end of the session or have a chat in the office or a cuppa in the parents' room. If a parent needs a family nursery nurse's attention the teacher quietly slips into the family group waiting to be served lunch. Parents are always given time, even at the busiest time of the day. From time to time a parent joins their child for lunch or tea. Every parent is

expected to have lunch with a child for the first time. Mothers in the
nearby homeless family unit often spend the day in the nursery rather
than return to the cemetery where the unit was based. A meal is provided either in the nursery with their children or they enjoy a pleasant lunch in the parents' room. The cook is always helpful and we
never charge for the meal.

Appearance as an aspect of environment

Our main priority was to help families overcome their insecurity and
anxiety about institutions and professionals. We used christian
names and our dress was informal. When I first arrived at the Centre
I was presented with a large white plastic badge with my name and
my designation clearly printed. Nursery nurses wore blue check
nylon overalls, students purple ones, cooks yellow ones, cleaners
green ones, all clearly labelled. Teachers and the Matron and
Head did not wear overalls. This pattern of overt hierarchy and
knowing your place was quite destructive and distasteful when
comfortable clothing to do the job properly was more important.
Lifting chunky equipment, changing nappies, playing with clay,
and sand, glue and paints, lying on the floor with trains and
blocks – all these activities relied on wearing easy care clothing.
Trousers were so practical. Shorts and sandals in the summer
were welcomed. The idea was to enjoy the work as well as offer
enjoyable experiences to the children and families. Soon all staff
shared the play, indoors outdoors, the messy jobs and the laundry
chores. This resulted in visitors and new parents being unsure
on a first visit who was staff, student or parent. The common
reply to a visitor seeking the Head was 'Have you looked in the
sandpit'?

Such informality clearly presented problems at times. Staff soon
relied on the Head and Matron's daily contribution in helping them
with the children and the parents. There were times when it was
difficult to reduce their presence in every day chores and enable them
to fit in their specific work.

How did this family atmosphere develop? What types of organisation were worked through which created clear lines for better
relationships between parent and staff?

The Family Group

The Centre was generously staffed to ensure that with good planning and regular evaluation, the needs of all should be adequately met. We recognised that a large proportion of referred children had special needs. We were aware of the importance of emotional and social maturity. We felt that emotional security could be established in several ways, in the organisation and quality of care, and in the commitment of staff. Staff began to accept that they must work towards a greater involvement and interaction with families.

So that children could function effectively in a large class of up to thirty children, we organised the children into small social groups called Family Groups. Each nursery nurse had a group of three children in the Baby Den and between seven and ten in the older nursery. Some of these children attended on a full-time basis throughout the year. The Family Group provided an opportunity for the child to be gradually introduced into the routine with a small intimate group of children, within a larger class, in a busy, confusing Nursery Centre. It offered a close relationship with one adult so that the child could identify with that adult. On entering the Centre the child received a warm welcome. When settling in, in the first few weeks, she received consistent affection, encouragement and support. When distressed, tired or unwell she would usually be comforted by her nursery nurse who offered a substitute mother figure.

The Family Group helped to give the child a sense of identity. She began to identify with 'my' group. The group fostered consistent care in a Centre with a staff who worked shifts. It offered stability and group activities with a familiar group of children which helped to develop confidence, social skills and cooperation. The group encouraged close relationships with peers and sometimes intimate friendships, so necessary for single children, and children with unhappy experiences at home. The integration of children requiring fuller day care and children with a range of handicap and disability, playing and living with more fortunate children extended the value of the Family Group even more. It offered opportunities for older and younger children, able and disabled, to observe a range of behaviour, to be exposed to a variety of language and play and to develop at a pace appropriate to them. When children identify and experience security and stability, their development both intellectual and cognitive is more easily fostered and enriched.

The value of the family group to parents

Parents were often anxious and insecure when their child started at the Centre. They saw a large group of children, and unfamiliar adults and they looked around hopefully for a friendly face. As each nursery nurse had a small group of children in her care, it was easier for her to relate to parents daily. The Family Group offered the parent security too and it helped to form friendship and trust between the staff and parent. Parents could be advised and encouraged by the staff who knew their children well. This trust led to more involvement by the parents in the routine of the Centre by helping on the rota each week, joining outings and family group activities.

The Baby Den

It is essential to acknowledge at the outset, that in our experience, caring for the very young child for long periods during the first three years of life, in groups, with a variety of adults and in an artificial setting, is not the ideal way to fulfil their needs and promote their optimum development. For the great majority of children whose early years are spent in this way, it is by reason of necessity rather than by parental choice. This seemingly simplistic judgement has been strongly influenced by close observation of children, staff and parents and is tempered by the care available.

When children are admitted under the age of three, it is generally because alternatives have failed, and parents are perhaps unable to cope with the demands of parenthood. Having recognised and accepted an ever present dilemma in matching theory and practice, our task in establishing quality day care was to:

(a) minimise the possible damaging effect of nursery life on a small child.
(b) exploit all the resources available for the benefit of the child.
(c) capitalise on all the advantages of staff involvement with the family.

The first and most important hurdle to overcome was separation from the parents. Unless it was essential, we did not offer full-time places, five days a week. Thus we wanted to share the responsibility for the child with the parents, rather than take it from them and possibly reinforce their inadequacies. In our experience, two or three days or four mornings or two afternoons was sufficient to relieve the pressure in the home and still allow the child to maintain some daytime experience with the family. Where necessary, of course, the single parent who needed to work was offered a full-time place. Yet our experience revealed the need for more support in the home as most of our single parents found coping with work and a family too demanding.

Most of our children were referred by Health Visitors and Social Workers. Once it was established that a place was available our 'mini-visit' routine began. Parents were asked to bring their children everyday during the week prior to admission on their selected days. They could come during the morning or afternoon and usually stay up to two hours each session. During this time many encounters took place, which were a preparation for future relationships.

They were exposed to a new environment with often unfamiliar equipment and materials. They observed and hopefully interacted with new and unfamiliar adults and children. Nothing positive may have seemed to be happening. The parent may slump in a despondent stupor, wondering 'how all this can possibly help'. They may be bursting with irritation and longing to just leave the child and go. Sometimes, of course, parents refused or could not manage to arrange preparatory visits, but this was rare.

Towards the end of the week, the parent and child had lunch with us. The parent also withdrew to the Parents' Room occasionally for short periods so that staff could assess how this affected the child and the parent. We took plenty of time in incidental chat with the parent which helped to build up the trust which must exist between us if we were to work together successfully.

Usually separation from the parent was achieved painlessly for them both after this week of introduction and we shortened the first few sessions where necessary. Occasionally difficulties did occur, but we usually were able to assess whether a child was really distressed or protesting for effect. Some children did benefit from a period of four to six weeks full-time attendance before it was reduced to the part-time allocation. This usually occured when the children had little experience of regular routine and needed time to adjust to the pattern of the day. Once a child was happily settled, parents were encouraged to spend time in the Baby Den at anytime of the day and for as long as they choose to stay.

The majority of children referred to the Baby Den were between the age of one year and eighteen months. This is a crucial period when the rate of development is very rapid. The normal child recognises himself as an individual with very positive needs. He is beginning to express himself in a number of ways and recognises the adult as the person to answer his need – immediately and continuously. He is mobile and recognises that the world is there to be explored – on feet, on hands and knees or bottom shuffle. The great difficulty for children at this age is their inability to recognise the rights and needs of others. They have not yet learnt to share, take turns, to wait or be left. The child's demands for himself are paramount. When this potential volcano is introduced to the Centre he joins a group of about ten children, aged nine months to about three years, all of whom have additional problems related to their home situation.

Each nursery nurse had an observation group of about six children through the week. Most of the children in the unit attended only two or three days a week, this allowed the staff to work in depth with a maximum of three children each at any one time, promoted observation and eased the competition for the adult's attention. It is unwise to encourage children to become too attached to one adult in a team. Thus each session usually has no more than ten children with three or four trained staff in the Baby Den.

The lack of essential facilities for the youngest children led us to assume that the original planners did not envisage much demand for the care of babies and toddlers still in nappies. There was no adequate bathing, changing or sluicing facilities (in the early years) and funds had to be raised by parents to improve the bathroom facilities. The siting of the sluice and the laundry and changing facilities were inadequate but staff accepted these areas as stress areas and endeavoured to minimise the stress for the children by careful handling.

The open plan design of the building was created to encourage the integration of the under threes with the older children. So that one year olds could join a family group. Shortly after opening the Centre it became obvious that the facilities and layout of play areas was unsuitable for the youngest children's needs.

It is better if the youngest children are grouped together in the care of a number of nursery staff in their own home base and with their own facilities, but still with many opportunities for integrating their play and social contacts with older children when appropriate. Various experiments were tried, including the Playcourt (see Figure 5.1), until a home base was established in a quiet den off a main nursery play area.

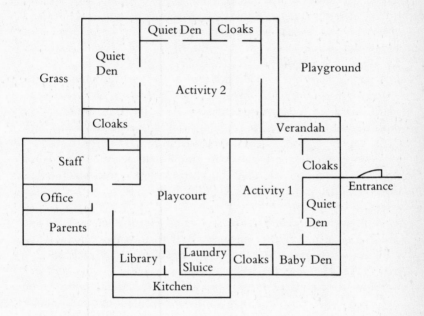

Figure 5.1 Plan of centre
Note: Not to scale.

Although this quiet den was small and had many drawbacks, it was actually the only room with a window facing the surrounding streets. This offered oportunities to maintain contact with the outside world, and was used by the staff to focus the chldren's attention on everyday happenings; the children walking to school, the dustbin lorry tipping up, the delivery of coal for the boilers, the bus moving up the hill and so on.

To expect to create the atmosphere of a typical family living room in an office building, with its grey plastic walls, was probably a little ambitious. Yet the Baby Den Staff introduced many attractive touches to the children's immediate environment. Wallpaper panels on some of the display areas, plants hanging from the ceiling, gay fabrics for curtains, cushions and covers and several armchairs donated from homes all helped to create a welcome.

Sadly for some of the Baby Den children, the play area was not a poor substitute for home. Settling into the nursery environment presented real cultural differences. Children had to adjust to a clean, warm, attractive and stimulating environment, with routines and order, regular meals, sleeping patterns and new expectations of behaviour. Adults were interested in them, had time and patience and enjoyed their company.

A busy school kitchen was not the ideal place into which to take the under threes, but since an outdoor playspace was situated next to a large kitchen window, the babies were able (with the aid of a set of boxsteps) to follow the progress of a sack of carrots, from delivery to the vegetable dish. This compensated in some way for the lack of experience in ordinary domestic routine which they should have had at home. Lunch time cleaners and visiting workmen contributed to this continual process of bringing the necessary contact to the restraints of day care.

Meals were presented in as near a family setting as possible. The children sat usually in the same place, at the same small table with the same staff sharing a meal presented attractively, with tablecloths, cutlery, mugs and adult serving crockery. A child having a nursery lunch for the first time would normally have a parent sitting beside and eating with her. An example of some difficulties can be drawn from the situation of a child normally eating his meals on the floor with his fingers in the company of the family dog. In the nursery he was expected to sit quietly at a table on a chair, using utensils with interested adults chatting to him as well as taking his turn and waiting to be served or offered some more.

Parents often found this a difficult situation, especially if the home eating routine was vastly different from that of the Centre. Consequently, gentle easy introductions to nursery meals were not always possible but most parents were pleased to have an opportunity to share in 'what goes on' at mealtimes. Children's feeding difficulties were discussed daily with their parents so that progress could be recognised or home difficulties could be taken into account and staff allow for regressive stages dominated by home stress.

The child who was still small enough to sleep in a cot or pram could still be catered for individually, to rest when needed and in relative quiet, and in similar situations as offered at home. The older children could not be offered an individual sleeping pattern as the facilities were so limited. A sleeping area had to be created each day in a quiet den in another part of the Centre, with canvas beds arranged in dormitory style. We tried to ensure that the Den staff were there when a child awoke, especially when children were new, and other staff working near the sleep area always alerted them to waking children.

In a building where the activities within it had long ago completely outgrown the space and facilities provided and which in the prevailing economic climate seemed unlikely to be expanded, it was continually surprising that new developments did take place. It was very encouraging to notice that far from feeling defeated by the limitations of the building, staff were eager to cater for individual needs and flexibility of Centre provision was manipulated with great expertise.

Staff Responses

In the early years at the Centre there was a noticeable rivalry for responsibility between the teacher and the nursery nurse. One of the first challenges was to clarify the position of teacher and nursery nurse. There is so much overlapping in their work with young children. We firmly established the role of the nursery nurse as crucial to the sound emotional and social development of young children in group care. Her responsibility for a small Family Group provided her with a recognised position of authority in a larger group of children and the support of a team leader.

The Family Group also provided the nursery nurse with less stressful training situations with only a few full-time children in her care. Thus toilet training, bathing and meal times were closer to family type relationships with the nursery nurse. It was also easier for the nursery nurse to form trusting relationships with a small number of parents, listening to problems, advising, sharing and cooperating to ensure the security necessary for fostering good emotional development.

As the role of the nursery nurse was for the child's emotional and social development, the teacher had more opportunity to concentrate on enabling the child's intellectual progress. The Family Group offered the teacher the opportunity to plan individual children's programmes with the nursery nurse. The teacher was also able to support her colleague at stressful times such as mealtimes, particularly when very disturbed children upset and disrupted and diverted the nursery nurses's attention from the other children.

What were the staff feelings about this development in their work and the sharing of responsibility? How did they adapt their practice and develop their individual skills? What were some of the most pressing demands?

> I have had to come to terms with parent involvement with the children in the nursery.

> I don't think I have changed my ideas about working with children generally, but I feel I have been made to think more deeply watching staff show more understanding and tolerance and giving more help to parents than I have ever encountered before. I have had to adjust to it being no longer just a job but a commitment.

> There were things I had to change; the pace of working sometimes due to poor concentration and language skills, leaving some things if another child needs attention, giving time to children.

> I have always tried to provide a caring and consistent relationship with children, but I have had to change the way I go about it. I no longer see the child in isolation from the family. I am now very aware of starting where the child is 'at' and not where I think it should be. I observe more and think about what is happening. I know I need a nonjudgemental attitude towards parents to encourage their confidence and trust.

> I needed to modify my own role and practice acquired in training, by delegating to others and by using the expertise, commitment and interests of those with whom I worked so closely. This was not an easy task and did not happen overnight. I had to adjust to working closely with a team of three nursery nurses and a part-time teacher. In teaching practice I only ever worked with one nursery nurse.

Having a child grow so fond of you that she will not let you out of her sight for a moment. I had been at the Centre only six weeks and felt my training had been pretty useless.

I have found the most challenging demand has been made by the full-time children. The greatest challenge is to try to help a child settle into a group but still make it feel like an individual who matters.

Dealing with very disturbed children and caring for new children, settling them into nursery life.

Counselling parents and devising programmes for children with severe developmental problems.

I found I had to adjust to an expectation of communication and involvement with parents.

It was essential to develop a team of skilled staff who could respond to parents. There were some parents with serious problems and with children who had been seriously injured non accidentally, who were emotionally scarred, were rejected, were handicapped, were either withdrawn or alternatively wild and undisciplined. Most were from single parent homes, some with adult support, many without.

CHAPTER 6

Early childhood education

Play, which provides suitable opportunities to strengthen the body, improve the mind, develop the personality and acquire social competence, is therefore as necessary for a child as food, warmth and protective care.

(Mary Sheridan 1977)
(Spontaneous Play
in Early Childhood).

'We want to learn him'

This phrase was commonly voiced by parents when they came to put their child's name down on the waiting list. For some parents this learning was interpreted as discipline, others were anxious for a chance for their children to play and socialise with other young children. Many wanted their child to gain independence 'and stand on his own feet', which included coping with new adults and experiences outside the house. Yet the majority of families who had thought about nursery education and had involved their children in toddler group and playgroup, believed that the Centre would most importantly prepare their child for school. This expectation focused their high hopes for the child to do well at school, perhaps better than they had. It centred on the child learning to read and doing 'his numbers' as early as possible to give him a good start in the infant class. Thus a great challenge for Centre Staff was to establish high standards in learning opportunities for children aged under 1 year old to 5 years 4 months.

Recent research in education, sociology and psychology has moved nursery teachers to consider more seriously their role as educationalists. Nursery education has tended to be developed in areas of serious disadvantage. The evidence from the American Headstart programmes combined with the Educational Priority Areas scheme following the Plowden Report, began to clarify the potential of a well planned nursery education programme. It became more clear that the nursery staff had a challenge to intervene more successfully in educational disadvantage by placing more emphasis on cognitive and linguistic growth, working more closely with parents and providing a range of structured and carefully designed programmes of play to meet the individual children's needs, in particular those with handicaps and learning difficulties. Margaret Donaldson offered teachers more insight into how young children's minds develop and how they learn. Kathy Sylva and her team in the Oxford Research Project provided a fascinating reappraisal of how children play and how nurseries function. Joan Tough's Project on Communication Skills offered nursery teachers and nursery nurses more evidence, guidance and training opportunities to consider the use of language and how to foster communication skills in young children. The Nuffield Mathematics Teaching Project and Geoffrey Matthew's work on early mathematical experiences inspired nursery staff to extend their perception of the value of first hand experiences in play which offered opportunities for grasping the vital early concepts in problem solving and logical thought: David Weikhart's Longitudinal study in Ypsilanti with pre-schoolers is now providing further evidence of the value of quality pre-school education in tackling educational disadvantage and helping young children retain its benefits into adolescent life.

The precarious situation of nursery education as an economic pawn in the politics of the day also led us to consider society's views on our expertise as teachers. Frequently we were called on to defend or even justify our existence to politicians, the public and even our colleagues in statutory education. The rise of the playgroup movement and the increasing support it received from government and local authorities in periods of economic depression as an alternative to nursery schooling further increased the pressure on nursery teachers. What was the teacher's role as she worked closely with a larger number of nursery nurses who had also received a particular training to work with young children? The NFER had produced a very useful report on the aims, role and deployment of staff in the nursery and in particular support the team leader role of the nursery teachers to ensure continuity in an extended day and throughout the year. This chapter is concerned with the way in which we worked through the principles and out towards the practice. Participation of all nursery staff in the planning is essential.

Planning was crucial to the development and continuity of learning situations presented at the Centre. There were three teams with four adults and some students in each team. The teams worked a shift system with staggered holidays. The children were vertically aged in small family groups of 3–5 year olds as part of a larger class unit. There was a wide social mix of families with a high proportion of disadvantage and handicap. Pupils from the local comprehensive schools worked regularly with us for up to six weeks at a time and parents were involved incidentally in the classrooms as well as more formally on weekly rotas as members of the teams.

Much of our work was guided by Piaget's research. We believed that children learn by doing; by exploring their environment; through questioning and discussion. Their interest first had to be aroused so the nursery environment had to be stimulating and interesting. Our children gradually gained knowledge and understanding as they accumulated and reconciled the information through their direct and first hand experiences. We therefore accepted that language and communications skills were of prime importance. We reasoned that an adult depends on language to fulfil the teaching role and children must listen, interpret, question and demonstrate understanding and express their thinking in language. Talking is the main means of communication in the early years.

From an early stage it became essential to draw staff's attention to the need to observe their practice. The Head and Matron spent much of their time observing in their first year of appointment in the nursery. They watched how children played indoors and outdoors, how they coped with some of the restrictive space. They watched the changing patterns of behaviour, the opportunities for group interaction or quiet, reflective solitary play. There was an essential period of observation of staff skills and strengths, their planning procedures, their assessment and evaluation techniques. During this period of close observation, too, the two senior staff played with the children, humped equipment and furniture around with the rest, joined staff in group activities and demonstrated their own personal strengths and

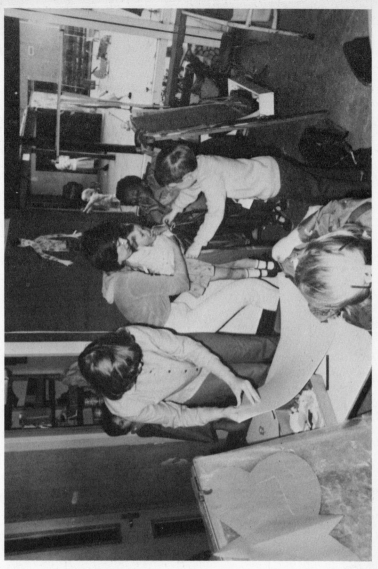

The busy nursery environment

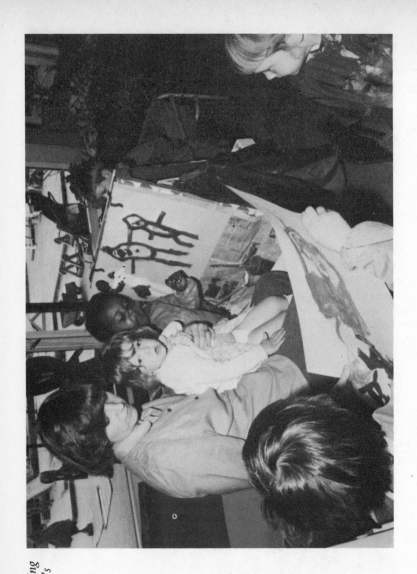

Responding, discussing and sharing children's work

standards. Following this period of evaluation discussions then were arranged to extend the staff perspective on planning the environment and meeting individual children's needs.

When planning the learning experiences for children, staff needed to observe critically and evaluate the provision of time, space and materials relevant to the activities, and to assess which activities met the needs and stages of development of the children, participating in them either in groups or as individuals.

It was vital to assess whether sufficient time was offered for play. If there was a keen interest in an activity should it be offered again during the afternoon session or the following morning? If there was a lack of interest in an actvity should it be changed completely or modified? Staff had to observe which children needed prior warning that an activity was soon to end so that they were not too engrossed or dismayed at having to stop. Alternatively observation indicated which children required extra time for specific activities and which children should not be interrupted when engrossed in the activity.

In a large open plan building it was essential to consider the flexibility and organisation of space for safe play activity. Observation revealed errors in presentation of activities, suggested new positioning, taking floor space, height of tables and child perspective and numbers of bodies into consideration.

The range of activities and the equipment was enormous. Staff constantly observed their availability, quality, regular and irregular use, adaptability and condition.

Observation of the children was essential in assessing their stage of development, identifying delay and handicap, particular learning difficulties such as poor concentration, communciation skills, and special needs, physical, emotional and social. Teachers wanted to identify the initiators of play activities, the leaders and the followers who may require extra help to maintain their self confidence and feeling of security. Staff had to observe the right time and place for beneficial intervention, in disputes as well as asking questions and leading the children into more complex learning situations and problem solving.

Planning the children's learning experiences

Much of the work at the Nursery Centre was introducing children to new experiences, a broader, more complex environment and a wider range of adults and peers groups. The nursery experience was not a short cut to further educational success. We hoped it would lay a firm foundation for later progress but our concern was its impact on our children at the time they attend the Centre. Any beneficial long term effects were a bonus and would depend on the interaction between parent, Centre and the primary schools. We were helping children to acquire skills and knowledge. As children grasp the meaning of new materials and acquire new concepts, they should begin to apply the information to new situations confidently

The teaching staff met regularly over a period of weeks to consider and clarify their roles as teachers at the Centre. They needed to establish their aims and consider what they hoped young children could achieve intellectually during their attendance at the Centre. They considered the essential learning experiences to enable the children to achieve their intended objectives, including the necessary skills, the activities, their resources and the classroom organisation and method. Then followed some consideration of assessment techniques to check whether the children were achieving what was hoped for. Regular evaluation of the teaching input resulted in the gradual evolution of expertise in individual and group teaching techniques relevant to a changing group of young children who might attend the Centre full-time for up to 50 weeks of the year, or attend part-time during school terms only.

After careful consideration, plenty of discussion, alternating despondency and confidence with the task, we accepted our need to be realistic and therefore view our aims on children's intellectual development as a starting point, and ideally, a direction in which to proceed with our regular planning of the daily routine.

The working party produced the following guideline in diagram form for convenience, to regularly refer to, and to give all new staff to help them understand the policy. These guidelines were for all staff to work with including the Baby Den staff with the youngest children. The Guidelines are reproduced here as Figures 6.1, 6.2, 6.3 and 6.4.

Figure 6.1 Objectives to consider to foster intellectual development.

EXPLORING

a. by providing a stimulating environment.
b. by offering plenty of time to participate.
c. by offering encouragement and praise.

MANIPULATING

a. by developing sensory skills (e.g. tasting touching etc.)
b. by developing eye and body co-ordination
c. by increasing finer and gross motor skills.

INVESTIGATING

a. by reasoning logically
b. by interacting with adults
c. by interacting with peers
d. by expressing themselves in speech or action

OBSERVING

a. by developing his ability to attend
b. by concentrating

LISTENING

a. by receiving information
b. by interpreting information
c. by interacting with adults
d. by interacting with peers.

EXPERIMENTING

a. by handling unfamiliar materials
b. by repetition
c. by discovering properties
d. by understanding properties

DISCUSSING

a. by exchanging ideas
b. by extending language skills
c. by responding to verbal instructions
d. by offering verbal instructions
e. by working co-operatively

Figure 6.2 Skills to develop.

For exploring
a. Crawling
b. Climbing
c. Balancing
d. Swinging
e. Choosing
f. Hanging
g. Splashing
h. Digging
i. Banging
j. Poking
k. Squeezing

Manipulating
a. Tasting
b. Touching
c. Smelling
d. Hearing
e. Seeing
f. Fitting
g. Screwing
h. Building
i. Steering
j. Catching
k. Throwing
l. Pushing
m. Pulling
n. Loading

Observing
a. Looking
b. Thinking
c. Assimulating
d. Deciding
e. Waiting
f. Attending

EXPERIMENTING
a. Constructing
b. Building
c. Designing
d. Co-operating
e. Adjusting
f. Relating
g. Destroying

LISTENING
a. Hearing
b. Concentrating
c. Relating
d. Thinking
e. Talking
f. Remembering
g. Discriminating
h. Interpreting

DISCUSSING
a. Talking
b. Arguing
c. Commenting
d. Suggesting
e. Thinking
f. Relating
g. Directing
h. Persuading
i. Encouraging
j. Accepting
k. Assimulating
l. Repeating
m. Answering
n. Instructing
o. Reasoning
p. Imagining

INVESTIGATING
a. Asking
b. Talking
c. Thinking
d. Relating
e. Remembering
f. Comprehending
g. Enquiring
h. Concentrating
i. Relating
j. Assimulating
k. Classifying
l. Ordering
m. Comparing
n. Counting
o. Reporting
p. Identifying
q. Conserving
r. Predicting
s. Completing
t. Solving

Figure 6.3 Skills, activities and resources.

SKILLS	ACTIVITIES	RESOURCES
	Walks	Parks
For EXPLORING	Picnics	– Town
	Visits	Shops
		Community Resources, (Library, Fire Station, Post Office)
		Farm
		Forest
	Swimming	Swimming Pool
	Paddling	Paddling Pool
For DISCUSSING	P.E.	– Water Trough
		Bath
		Bathroom (i.e. Wash hand basin, toilet)
		Climbing Apparatus
	Movement	Tapes, Records
	Drama	Percussion, Homecorner
	Fantasy Play	Radio, Dressing up clothes
	Music	Piano, guitar, voice
For QUESTIONING	Stories	– Books, puppets, pictures, Props
		Drawing pen and paper
	Games	– Commercial and Improvised Games
	Cooking	– For special and other occasions at home and nursery
	Nature Study	– Garden, animals, woods, fields, parks etc.
For LISTENING	Displays	– Books, natural phenomena, children's work
	Finger Plays	Puppets, objects,
	Visual Aids	– Flannelgraph
	Humans	– OURSELVES, Doctor, nurse, policeman, fireman, builder, roadman.
For OBSERVING	Drawing	– Different media – pencils, crayons, felt pens, charcoal.

SKILLS	ACTIVITIES	RESOURCES
	COOKING	– Rolling pins, Cutters, Boards, tins, trays, Oven, food Ingredients
For MANIPULATING MATERIALS	GARDENING	– Seeds, Plants, Carrots tops etc, trough, gardens, garden tools, wheelbarrow, watering cans, canes, string.
	PAINTING	– Easel, Table, Finger, feet, paint brushes, pots, paper card etc.
For EXPERIMENTING	MODEL MAKING	– Junk materials, glue, spreaders, scissors
	PICTURE MAKING	– Junk materials, wool, paper shells, foods, scissors, glue spreaders
	MODELLING	– Clay, sand, plasticine, dough, tools, cutters
For OBSERVING	WOODWORK	– Scraps of wood, broken equipment, nails, hammer, bench, glue, saw, sandpaper
	SMALL CON-STRUCTION	– Puzzles, lego, mobilo, constructor straws, beads, meccano, connector playpax farms set, road and harbour set
For INVESTIGATING	LARGE CON-STRUCTION	Bricks, sand, blocks, – curtains, planks, boxes, wheels, ladders, steps
	WATER PLAY	– Bottles, containers, pipes, hoses, junk bottles, water bottles, bowls, baths, jugs, graded containers, sponges, shells, stones, magnets, straws.
	WHEELED TOYS	– Prams, tractors, cars, dumper, train, 'bikes, trolleys, caterpillar.
	MAKE AND MEND	– Old irons, kettles, clocks, bits of car engine, screwdrivers, hammers.

Figure 6.4 Fostering language.

AIM

1. We hope that all children will acquire the ability to express themselves in simple terms.
2. We hope that they will develop the ability to respond to simple verbal instructions.

HOW WILL THIS BE ACHIEVED?

a. By developing listening skills.
b. By observing
c. By responding to other children
d. By responding to adults
e. By encouraging and extending language skills:
        vocabulary and labelling
        sentence making
        expression
        questioning
        logical reasoning
        predicting
        projecting
        understanding speech
        reporting past and present experiences
f. By enjoying language.

The learning experiences essential to foster these skills can only be offered and developed by adult/child interaction. Observation of the children's use of language, assessing their grasp of the use of language, and the regular verbal communication with them should enable staff to provide the widest range of experience to meet the needs of the least able and the most able child.

General Aims for Intellectual Development

1 It is hoped that all children will develop a deep curiosity for their environment.
2 It is hoped that all children will acquire the ability to respond to verbal instructions.
3 It is hoped that they will develop the ability to respond to verbal instructions.
4 It is hoped that the children will achieve some basic understanding of mathematical and scientific concepts.
5 It is hoped that they will develop some practical knowledge to enable them to solve problems.

These aims and objectives were prepared for a full staff meeting discussion. They were not considered for the sole use of teaching staff. They were made available for reference for new ideas, for revitalising stagnant practice, establishing a varied learning programme, for aiding planning for specific skills and knowledge by the team. It was however recognised that the teacher had the responsibility to plan the environment and the individual children's programmes with the team of nursery nurses, to provide a rich and stimulating range of activities and resources, to foster cognitive skills, and promote language and communication skills. Each member of the team had specialist skills and knowledge. Only by working closely together, with regular discussion, planning and evaluation could these aims be achieved.

The work in the classroom

The following account of a team approach to the needs of the children, expertise of the staff, evaluation of the learning process and clarification of roles and responsibility, is presented by a teacher who had worked for two and a half years at the Centre, who had never had to work in a large team situation or been involved in shift work.

In the early days at the Centre the activities offered each morning were almost set out at random, but it became clear that as staff were on shifts and the room was prepared before the teacher arrived that a clear plan of the day and the week was needed, which avoided over or under use of activities and materials. The teacher needed to prepare a weekly plan of activities with members of the team who could change an activity at any time if they felt the needs of the children demanded it. This weekly plan was not rigid. It was flexible to accommodate immediate interests presented by a child. Some sessions had a definite theme, for example, transport. The activities would then follow this interest through:

Printing with paint and transport shapes and templates.
Clay with junk materials and wheels for modelling.
Transport dominoes . . . group game.
Puzzles with a transport theme.
Floor area with bricks and cars, lorries planks etc.
Sand with roads, cars, garage etc.
Water with boats and playpeople.

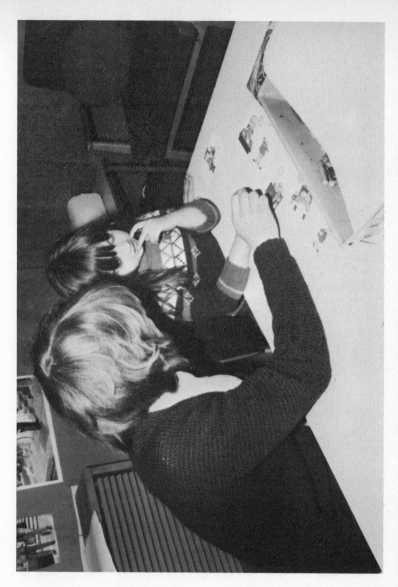

Essential individual attention

*Concentration and
creativity*

If there was no particular theme the activities would offer a range of cognitive and tactile experiences with imaginative play in the home corner area.

There was a table for creative activities each session. this area was shared by all the team, who took it in turns to plan and supervise the activity. When curtain activities lost their appeal to children and were abused or neglected, for example sand, water or, clay, the team discussed and exchanged ideas for the neglect and ways of renewing interest.

Working to a Theme

Of course it was not necessary or desirable to work to a theme all the time. Firstly many of our children were too young or immature to sustain interest and we could have become a rigid organisation unable to meet individual staff and children's needs. Yet at times we felt a theme linked our interests very successfully. The theme approach was discussed at the weekly team meeting. Staff made a variety of suggestions until one theme was agreed upon. Each staff took a particular aspect and developed it with her family group. The teacher sometimes developed it in more depth with the older children. All staff promoted the theme in a variety of activities offered to all the children. The weekly plan was therefore essential to help staff on different shifts arrange the activities around their arrival and departure. A great deal of thought was put into the arrangement of the room and activities. Although the room was quickly disturbed by the arrival of children, we hoped that if it was attractively set out it would stimulate their interest to more positive play.

The early observations revealed that with a wide choice of play many children were not using the opportunities offered. At this stage we reconsidered the arrangement of furniture. The playroom was a very awkward shape with six exits and a large plate glass window along one side. Many of our children had poor concentration spans, were very active, often easily over stimulated and excited. To arrange quiet, nondistracting areas as well as messy and active areas was quite a challenge if each area was going to be easily accessible and well supervised. One reappraisal of the working area produced the following:

A table area with a trolley beside which had a selection of equipment on it, for children to choose freely from.

A floor area where children could play undisturbed.

Some tables facing the wall where children could play with their backs to the many distractions in a busy playroom.

Several areas where children could sit quietly and relax with books.

A quiet comfortable area for parents where they could relax and observe their children or read and have coffee.

The design of the room undoubtedly influenced and often restricted the work. The two quiet dens leading off the main classroom had curtains across the doorways. We wanted to erect a sliding door across one entrance to provide a truly quiet area for family group work and a range of individual and other small group activities. This was never achieved.

It was important to establish a routine in the classroom which provided security for the staff and the children and promoted some continuity around the staggered holiday and shift pattern. The vulnerable stress periods in the day centred on the lunch break with half the children remaining in the Centre and a new intake of part-timers in the afternoon. Collecting children from the morning and afternoon sessions during the clearing away of activities and the preparation of meals required considerable thought to ease the noise, movement and safety of children and adults. Chores had to be shared by the whole team and opportunities for consultation with parents at these difficult times acknowledged whilst the quality of involvement with the children was maintained.

Throughout the debate on the children's intellectual development there was the firm commitment towards the value of play. There has been much criticism of nursery staff supervising play and rarely participating in the activities with the children. This was a well founded criticism as we observed in the early years. The outside environment provided many examples of strolling supervising adults, possibly chatting in pairs keeping an eye on the children and only intervening in disputes, usually over a tricycle.

The early nursery pioneers placed a great emphasis on the outside play areas. Margaret McMillan designed a garden with places for

Play is fun

Play is sharing an experience

Play is serious work

children to explore and to hide, to plant seeds and to care for animals. At Kirkby the outside environment was one of the most sterile and unattractive play areas one could imagine. The Centre was L shaped with a tarmaced and paved area in the front of the L and a strip of poor grass at the back. There were no trees, no flowers, no pretty bushes or shrubbery. The fence was brown planks with some vicious thorn bushes planted in the front, probably selected for easy care by the playing fields department but quite inappropriate for young children. The grass area at the back of the building was dug up frequently in the first few years to provide services for a social services hostel and for the special school on the campus. There was no door leading from the nursery onto the grass area, so plans to create an imaginative outdoor environment were drastically affected by the need to carry very heavy equipment and furniture around the whole building or to pass it through windows. People who do not work in nurseries probably have little idea of the tiredness factor in lifting and carrying equipment. The outdoor storage units were tiny with high shelves. Boxes, barrels, steps, mats, planks, tyres, climbing equipment, trikes, scooters, wheelbarrows, balls, sand equipment and so on had to be stored sensibly for easy removal on the early shift. Inevitably the equipment was jammed in where there were spaces and the unlucky staff setting up in the morning had to duck when the door opened!

We tried hard to make the outdoor area more inviting for the children and adults. At first the sandpit provided was dangerous for babies and toddlers. It was placed in the centre of the paved area with no protective wall and was about 2 feet 6 inches deep. It was far too big to have a cover and so soiling by the many stray dogs was a problem. The wheeled toys careered around the sandpit and toddlers with baby walkers lumbered sombrely towards the gaping pit. We had to spend much time negotiating to have the sandpit filled in and a smaller one rebuilt in a more helpful situation. During this rebuilding, money was raised by parents and a retiring ancillary worker to purchase three trees which were planted in the paved area to provide some shade in the hot weather. The flat strip of grass was improved by buying some logs from the forestry commission and having them sited in a mound on the grass area. This mound of earth was provided by a sympathetic bulldozer driver who was preparing the field next to the Centre for a new housing estate. The playing fields department then kindly returfed the area. After much consultation, a strip of the grass was made available for a vegetable and flower patch for the children. It was far too small but at least there was an area for planting and picking and weeding and so on. More logs were placed on the grass for children to sit on, jump off and make dens near. However the playing fields workmen were not allowed to mow around them as this increased their time schedule. Staff had to promise to cut the longer grass around the logs with their own shears.

The challenge of the outdoor area is one many nursery staffs have yet to conquer. The time to plan and set out the apparatus combined with the need for large numbers of adults to be available to enjoy the activities with the children is a constant problem.

The summer months produced a particularly exhausting period for staff who were striving to create imaginative outdoor learning experiences. First, the regular indoor activities were carried outside to give children the maximum time out of doors. Water trolley and equipment, painting and creative activities, home corner equipment with large boxes of blocks, bricks, cars, trains and aeroplanes were placed under the inadequate verandah. The sandpit was carefully set out with perhaps a barrel, planks, ramp, wheelbarrows, hoses, miniature adult tools – spades and rakes one day. Another day it might be set out to create roads, harbours and ports with buckets, water containers, vehicles and so on.

The building apparatus could be set out in many challenging ways to give opportunities for swinging, crawling, balancing, jumping and sliding. It might change dramatically to a den, a castle, a bus going to the seaside for the day. Tents, blankets and wigwams helped to provide shelter, dark spaces, private places. Carrying out the paddling pool and filling it with water through the staff room window offered another essential experience for the children.

To create a suitable challenging outdoor environment every day takes at least ¾ of an hour if it is to be set up with care. Also, lock, stock and barrel, it had to be carried back and stored in the sheds and the nursery rooms each evening; nothing could be left out due to vandalism and theft. For some staff this was a chore. It was heavy work and the setting up and clearing away occurred partly as children were arriving or being collected. Parents looked for staff to share a confidence but the moment might be lost because that key worker was humping ladders around to the back of the building. After much observation of the setting out and clearing up the outside area it became essential for the Head, Matron and the two deputies to take prominent roles. They were available on early and late shifts with the other staff and frequently provided the necessary backup in creating the learning experiences. They were particularly dominant in the early years in demonstrating how to play with children in the sandpit, in the block area, in the tent and in the tea-party under the verandah.

The winter months proved to be even more of a challenge. The senior staff expected children to explore the outside elements in poor weather. Puddles, mud, snow and blustery gales offered many exploratory experiences and occasions for laughter and conversation. The Forestry Commission woods nearby offered the twisting paths, shadowy undergrowth, changing seasonal colours and fruits which Margaret McMillan had so strongly worked for in Deptford. Yet the difficulties in encouraging staff and parents to wear and provide suitable clothing to enjoy these outings was often frustrating. Collections of warm children's clothing and wellingtons were made so that any child could be cosily dressed to combat the elements. Boots and wellingtons were provided for the staff. In the early years there was an underlying feeling of disapproval from some staff who hated the mess, the wind and the wet sand. A great deal of encouragement, demonstration and legpulling gradually won most staff over. Our training unfortunately is very institution orientated. Modern day living seems to have reduced many adults experiences of wet and cold weather walking. We had to undo some of the twentieth century style living which suggested cuddling up in the centrally heated lounge in front of the television as a more appropriate way of spending a wet afternoon. In our experience, if the children had wellingtons and suitable outdoor clothing the blustery wet afternoon offered endless investigations in puddles, streams and gutters. The feel of the wind, the noise of swirling autumn leaves and crackling sticks gave our children vital living sensations which enriched their experience and their vocabulary.

Kirkby is a mining town with few safe play spaces. Many families using the Centre had no private transport. Many of our children were in an institution all day and for a large amount of the year. One of our priorities 'to learn him' was to take children out of the Centre, often with parents to enjoy many basic first hand learning experiences. These outings helped parents understand the necessary experiences children needed which provided a firm foundation for intellectual growth, language and communication skills and group interaction.

During the term time we planned regular outings for each family group. This meant that a maximum of fifteen children with the family-group nursery nurse were able to enjoy a whole day away from the Centre. The part-time children obviously benefitted from the full day activity. The nursery teacher may have been involved or the Head or Matron. A number of parents would be invited to join them and there might be a student, an M.S.C. trainee or a secondary school pupil too. The outings varied in character but were all carefully planned to maximise the opportunities for social, recreational and intellectual growth. During the term in one nursery room investigating transport the three family groups opted to visit different types of vehicles. One group supplied with a picnic, buckets for sickness and many spare underpants, travelled down the motorway in the minibus to the East Midlands Airport. They were able to see aircraft, stationary and being refuelled, aircraft taxi-ing before take-off and hear the screech of landing wheels. They returned with posters, brochures and many photographs of the outing to be used in future discussions. Another group were taken to nearby Alfreton Station by the minibus. They purchased tickets and travelled to Nottingham on the train. The minibus collected them at Nottingham and a picnic took place in a park before returning to the Centre. Many other visits to shops, cafes, the library, the theatre, parks, the zoo, the farm, were regularly planned. Sometimes parents invited the family group to their house for biscuits and pop and to view the new litter of puppies or rabbits. Staff took groups of children to their homes, to play in the garden, have a picnic, pick apples, or bake a cake. There was a great deal of ingenuity and creative thinking applied to getting the children out of the institution.

The school holidays were even more important in extending these vital first hand experiences. The numbers of children reduced to 15–25. This created wonderful opportunities for even smaller group outings. The local primary school had an indoor learner swimming pool. It was never used in the holiday periods. We tentatively booked a few sessions a week which increased to every day, morning and afternoon. Four to five children could enjoy the water with high adult ratios. Babies and toddlers were just as excited by the water as the active four year old. Some of the children became very water confident well before starting school age. Picnics in the park, local woodlands and fields were regularly enjoyed. Outings into Derbyshire provided a new experience not only for the children and parents but for some staff. We took ropes and swings and ladders to tie in the trees. Children were stripped bare and paddled in the streams with fishing nets. A fire was built in the clearing and sausages cooked for lunch. Dough 'dampers' remembered in staff Brownie days were stickily wrapped around clean sticks and 'cooked' over the embers. Dens were made and insects closely examined. Sadly no fish were ever caught! These were the priority learning experiences held dear in our document to foster intellectual growth. The new skills acquired by the children were observed and recorded. New confidence and social interaction noted, and developed.

There were changes within the staff too. Some of their experiences were broadened and their confidence increased. They were given a great deal of personal responsibility which they all valued and responded to. Some insured their own car for use with the children. Others took the local authority minibus test and were able to borrow an Education, Social Services or Leisure Services minibus in Kirkby or nearby Sutton-in-Ashfield and Mansfield. Local comprehensive schools and a junior school were particularly helpful in lending their own minibus to the Centre during the holidays. The Head's husband had a P.S.V. Public Service Vehicle licence and drove the local community school coach. All this mobility opened up new experiences for the whole family, not only during the nursery sessions. Outings at the weekends were offered to extend some of the family experiences.

The pleasures surrounding this approach to learning were numerous. The flushed, sleepy child who described his afternoon on the return journey. The excited parent who enjoyed a new experience and wanted to share it with others back at the Centre. The exhausted staff who flung themselves down in the staffroom with a cuppa at the end of the day feeling satisfied and fulfilled in their work. The shared retelling of the outing with the Head or Matron or other staff whilst the pots were washed, and the wet pants put in the washing machine and the remains of the picnic discarded.

Such an approach to young children's learning relies on several factors. The first must be a deep commitment to children learning through experiences which challenge them intellectually accompanied by support and encouragement. The Head must provide the necessary resources such as vehicles and petty cash to match the enthusiasm and involvement of the staff. She must take risks in giving responsibility to young staff out of the establishment for a day. High staff ratios at the Centre fostered the approach but the Head had to help remaining staff undertake and respond to the extra workload when other staff are out 'enjoying themselves'. The involvement of parents was vital. For many parents learning was somthing to do with books, workcards, flashcards and sitting still at desks. We had a wonderful opportunity to share real learning with them and their children and, through sensitive discussion, help them recognise that they could and did provide experiences which prepared their children so well for the more academic approaches at a later stage. Using photographs and slides and cine cameras, these experiences could be shared with other families on display boards, in albums and books and on parent evenings and afternoons when a film could recall the fun, the interest and the concentration of learning out in the community.

The involvement of large numbers of staff required a commitment from them to meet regularly in order to plan their work effectively. In the early years this was a painful development, full of frustration. The major difficulty in the combined centre of communication between staff needed to be thoroughly thought out. The difficulty of meetings and consultation arose from the shift system and staggered holiday scheme. During the first year as Head of the Centre it was increasingly difficult to establish a regular time to meet staff when all would be present. We had to compromise on a number of issues. A full staff meeting was not possible on a weekly basis. After several attempts to create an expectation of regular staff meetings, we had to accept that a monthly meeting at the minimum could be developed and we had to accept that some staff would be on holiday or looking after the tea children.

Team Meetings

The planning of the children's learning programme and opportunities to discuss the children's progress and individual needs was essential on a more regular basis. Thus the weekly team meetings were devised. Each new term the Head met with each team in turn to share developments and problems. Then the teams met each week to consider the every day work in their area of the nursery. Although the four staff in a team worked closely throughout the day, it was imposssible to discuss problems and plan activities when involved with the children, parents and the students. Family situations changed rapidly and staff needed information to adjust sensitively to parent and child. As many parents were in the classroom throughout the day it was impossible to exchange information about families which others might hear. All the same, consultation, discussion and exchange of information was essential if a team approach was to develop. There had to be a commitment to sharing ideas, information and a joint approval of new approaches and plans. Gradually staff began to recognise their own needs for support, their need to develop skills and thier own importance as an individual within the group. They then became more prepared to meet weekly after their shift which could mean waiting nearly an hour before the meeting could begin.

Regular meetings definitely improved the working atmosphere in the team. If any member felt unhappy about anything they were encouraged to bring it up for discussion. Here was a challenging role for the teacher. Management of team meetings required skill. Sharing problems, criticisms, anxieties and relationship difficulties needed tact, patience and understanding. Uneasy relationships in the team were quickly apparent to parent and child and also affected other teams in the Centre. We gradually adopted a pattern for our meetings as follows:–

1 Information from the Head or other teams was passed on, regarding families, other agencies, etc.

2 Notices about events within the activity area or Centre were discussed, eg, Bonfire Party, Christmas activities, etc.

3 Discussion on the work in the classroom for the next week.

4 Children in the class. A range of discussion on particular children's needs. Each fortnight a Family Group was discussed and each child's development considered. Plans were shared for individual children and an assessment of the reasons for difficulties made which might result in a new plan to meet the need. This discussion sometimes revealed insufficient contact and support for a parent and our attention would then focus on this.

Shared discussion often revealed developmental delay in certain children which might have been overlooked in a class of thirty children. Later the teacher and nursery nurse responsible for the child discussed a particular approach or programme for the child. An example of this approach is the following:

> Child . . . 4 years old, attends part-time, very shy and withdrawn, rarely makes contact with other children, spends a lot of time walking about or gazing aimlessly into space. He is an only child, with contact only with his mother. Mother is tense and nervous and very houseproud.
>
> A list of activities would be selected during the week and the teacher and nursery nurse would take it in turns to draw the child towards the activity and play with him there. At other times they would encourage him to join another child and a group of children and stay with him to offer security in this obviously nervous situation. Where children rarely approach the messy activities a similar tactic would be used to encourage the exploration of these important materials.

Bruner's Oxford Research revealed many children 'cruising' in nursery rooms. These children spent much time on their own moving from one place to another, looking around and apparently searching for something to do, but unable to make a choice. Our discussions of each child frequently identified these children who were characteristically quiet, unobstrusive, non demanding. We sometimes realised that children who we thought were using the learning opportunities offered at the Centre would nevertheless be approaching entrance to school with a limited grasp of language, poor cognitive skills and unsatisfactory concentration and listening patterns. It was the responsibility of the teacher to lead discussions upon adjusting the routine to help these children who could not make appropriate use of the free play offered and needed a restricted environment at various times of the day. One approach was to develop a pattern of Family Group time which was usually the personal responsibility of the nursery nurse. Several times each week the Family Group met in the Quiet Den with the teacher and nursery nurse. A limited choice of activities was offered and all children were expected to tackle at least one activity and complete it. As there was a maximum of ten children with two adults in a quiet non-distracting environment, our most insecure children received intensive adult interaction with high expectation and direct teaching where necessary of the many skills which could be acquired through free choice play but which we were aware that they were missing.

The age range in the Centre areas could be from children aged four months up to children of almost five and four months. But there were certainly more younger children in the Centre at any one time than most teachers will have ever experienced. We realised during the early years that the needs of older children were often overlooked or not met until a satisfactory organisation had been evolved to meet those of the youngest. Work with older children in the open classroom was always accepted as good practice. However, noise levels, interruptions by younger children and open plan design difficulties led to the teaching staff discussing their observations of older children and the assessment of their cognitive and intellectual development often being lower than hoped for. It was agreed that the older children had specific needs which could be disturbed by continually playing in large open areas, with little direction and frequent interruption. There was only one room not in continual use in the building which had a door. This was the 'Library' created from the Matron's office when she moved into the Head's office. The room offered uninterrupted periods of quiet throughout the day. We therefore created a Fives group for the older children.

This Fives group was always organised by a teacher who used it to assess development and extend able children who needed longer periods of intensive activity, and it provided a small group situation in which the least able had an intensive input from the teacher. Most of the work in this group concentrated on acquiring language skills. Attention was given to improving listening skills, auditory memory, visual discrimination and fine motor skills. The work was extended by outings from the building to give the children more experiences in the community essential to their whole development. Individual language and speech programmes devised by the speech therapist were followed each day in sessions shared by the teacher and the nursery nurse.

Record Keeping

Records were kept of all the children in our care. They were kept by the teacher and nursery nurse and included the children's emotional and social development with relevant notes of home background along with their physical and intellectual development. Records were used regularly in team discussions when considering individual children's needs. A profile was then compiled for the use of the infant teachers. If our regular evaluation of children revealed little progress we were fortunate to be able to call in the agencies with more specific skills to extend our understanding and assist us where appropriate.

The intellectual growth of the youngest children

Throughout this chapter the philosophy of intellectual growth has been seen as an approach developed by all the staff. Yet we must pause to consider the needs of the very young children in a group setting and examine the approach, the personal contact and the explicit expectation of parental involvement in the much younger children's learning.

The Baby Den Staff planned their enviroment around the needs of children as young as a few weeks old up to three years of age. The inside area was tiny, cluttered yet full of warmth and laughter. The youngest child had their own facilities placed at their height and presented in a more homelike sittingroom environment. Sand was in a small baker's tray. Biscuit and sweet tins became containers for improvised equipment, much of which any house could devise. Shells, conkers, buttons, reels, cones, and so on could be sorted into different containers, shaken to create different sounds and classified into varying groups and sets. Soft toys, dolls, dressing up clothes, dough and plasticine were regularly available, with finger painting and clay an exciting messy experience, organised with large aprons, floorcloths and mops. Babies equipment was devised to stimulate visual discrimination, auditory sense and, of course, tactile experiences. Musical equipment was created with tubular bells, jingle bells on ankles and wrists and shakers and drums. The outside area was shared with the older children. We believed that the very young child required a home and garden situation with a few children and adults – not up to 60 children playing very noisily and actively, unaware of the tottering 18 month old close by.

We discovered that outside visits were more beneficial if they occurred in a similar way to a family outing. We tried to take the children out regularly, one adult with perhaps two children, for outings with ordinary essential experiences offered by the immediate environment. We did occasionally arrange a large outing with minibus but this is not the most appropriate way of meeting the needs of the youngest children. We were aware that many of the parents of these children could not provide outings with time to stand and watch a delivery van unload, or water rushing down the gutter into the drain, or investigate an interesting crack in the wall; so this was the very basic type of learning opportunity we wanted to present on our short outings, fitted anywhere into the day routine spontaneously.

After a few years we attempted to improve the outside play facilities for the under threes and alleviate, at least during the summer months, the pressures of a small indoor play-space. Money was raised to replace the second window in the playroom with an outside door, lay a paved patio, and fence off part of the original grassed area at the front of the nursery buildings. This was done by a Youth Opportunities Project with funds raised by discos, fêtes and jumble sales. Equipment suitable for younger children had been very difficult to arrange away from the larger, heavier and often more boisterous children. A separate time had been set at least once a day for sole use of the outside area by the Baby Den. Now the new play area for the Baby Den was improved, the range and type of appropriate play provision offered to the younger child in a more protected physical environment was increased. There was space for parents to sit comfortably outside to observe play that could occur in a small garden. Armchairs were carried out regularly and in good weather lunch was eaten outside.

As other agencies referred children with handicap and delayed development it was crucial to devise appropriate patterns of care and learning to assess the special needs of many under threes. One child, for example, was severely mentally and physically handicapped and came to the Centre at 14 months for several days each week. He lived some distance away and was transported in a Social Services taxi by the family aide. She was vital in maintaining links with the family, a mother and father of 18 years with mother pregnant again. This child required much supervision as he was inert and immobile at all times. Each day a regular pattern of physical exercise and stimulation was carried out, following the advice of the local physiotherapist. She visited each week to assess his developing spasticity and liaised with the paediatric assessment unit, the family, the health visitor and the social worker. She guided the key nursery staff in the regular routines of exercise. The teacher for the deaf visited to help us assess his hearing. Auditory discrimination programmes were devised and used daily. As there was no peripatetic teacher for the blind, we approached the social worker for the blind for help and dvice. She gave us the name of an inspiring outreach worker for the R.N.I.B. This lady lived in Birmingham but visited us on several occasions to guide and encourage us with the child's progress.

This was just one child in the Baby Den, out of 10, who required a very high level of staff involvement. Many of the youngest children had experienced or witnessed family violence, been moved into a series of flats and homes and were living with second or third father or mother figures or with grandparents. Our aims for helping these young children cope with their lives and benefit from the stimulating experiences throughout their stay at the Centre was devised by a working party of staff including those working with the babies up to the 5 year olds. We adopted them in the following document after several staff meetings:

We hoped that during their stay at the Centre all children would:

1 Establish sastisfactory relationships with adults, by experiencing a gradual introduction to nursery routine and unfamiliar adults, by approaching adults spontaneously, accepting strangers without stress and responding cooperatively to intervention, instruction and discipline.

This would be achieved by regular enjoyable interaction between adults and children, just and consistent handling and many opportunities to meet new people.

2 Establish satisfactory relationships with other children, by playing cooperatively in small and large groups, by not feeling overwhelmed by unfamiliar groups, by approaching and sharing activities already occupied by others.
3 Be able to cope with social situations such as mealtimes; by using utensils correctly, by introducing a variety of foods, by helping to prepare and clear away meals, by benefitting from the social intercourse at the table.

This would be achieved by attractive presentation, gradual introduction of acceptable standards with good examples set by the adult and opportunities to assist.

4 Be able to exercise self control, by taking turns, sharing, listening to others, giving way without loss of control and waiting patiently.

This would be achieved by consistency of staff discipline, giving children choices and opportunities for making decisions, which must include letting the children go 'too far'.

5 Gain a degree of independence; by separating happily from the parent, by adapting to a routine, by coping with mealtimes, bathroom management and dressing.

This would be achieved by observing the independence of older more capable children, by progressing through developmental stages at their own pace and by staff and parent praise and encouragement at all times.

6 Become self motivated and investigate; by enjoying the new experiences offered at the Centre, freely making use of the activities offered and exploiting the materials imaginatively.

This would be achieved by providing a rich environment to stimulate their curiosity, by staff anticipating the 'next step' and providing for it.

7 By developing a sense of security; by experiencing the gradual introduction to nursery routine, accepting a change in plan – a disappointment – an altered situation without difficulty and understanding known facts such as . . . mummy will come back, closed doors will open again, the family group nursery nurse is on holiday but will return next week and so on.

As we worked towards these objectives we acknowledged that children could only benefit from anything the Centre has to offer by understanding the level of their maturity. We accepted that some children reached the Centre severely damaged as a result of their family background or medical history. We had to be prepared to repair damage, and compensate for harmful experiences before we could hope for individual progress.

The constant challenge to the impact of nursery education on young children's development must rest with the commitment of the Staff, the clarity of their aims and objectives, and the quality of the care and education of the children linked to the participation and involvement of their parents in the experience.

CHAPTER 7

Parental involvement – the changing needs of families with young children

. . . . it's about women helping women.
                    (comment from a C.S.S. tutor to a nursery colleague).

The challenge of fostering a trusting relationship with families whose children are in day care, referred by agencies with supervision orders, and children on 'at risk' registers is great. The need to develop more sensitive, sympathetic attitudes between staff and family is matched by a growing awareness of skills and expectations of staff working in the pre-school field. The need to provide more comprehensive facilities for parents and children in order to facilitate involvement is also very evident.

The community in Kirkby was essentially white working class dependent on a limited range of employment which demanded a shift system, for both male and female employees. There was however a great deal of unemployment, depressive illness, marital stress and breakdown (in keeping with national trends). There remained a culture of extended family contact. But as grandparents were often young and in early middle age, the support expected was less evident; particularly that of the grandmother as she was often employed full-time in the local knitwear and hosiery firms. Thus we met an increasing number of young mothers, and sometimes young fathers, isolated, lonely, inexperienced in home-making and childcare, seeking support, advice, encouragement and friendship. Alongside these families with problems were families who were coping well with marriage, children and their employment. Often such parents, particularly the mothers who were happy to remain at home during their children's early years, were seeking outlets for their extra energy, social and educational talents. We considered social mix very important in the Centre.

Many parents used the facilities such as the Mother and Toddler Group, Toy Library, Childminders Support Group and Gingerbread even though their children did not attend the nursery. Our playspace, furniture and equipment was shared with these groups alongside our attempts to involve our children's families in the range of activities offered at the Centre.

Newsletters were printed each term with attractive covers, containing articles, illustrations and photographs prepared by staff, parents and other community workers. Posters, invitations to outings, meetings and workshops were attractively designed and displayed. These were designed by staff whose creativity had been noted and who had been encouraged to use their skills.

Parents were invited to join the team on a regular weekly basis for a session and to help in a variety of ways in the nursery room. They were not selected in any way.

Here is a teacher's account of a parent rota system:

> Parents who were interested were encouraged to come and spend a session each week with us. Although some would prefer to do odd jobs for us, many would eventually feel confident enough to play with the children. Before mothers started to help, I regularly spent some time discussing all the activities. Parents had a chance to discuss some of the fears they may have had over working alongside the staff. They usually ranged from a fear about their own child's reaction, to the disciplining of other people's children. We found that many parents became much more confident with the handling of their own child after they had helped on our rota for some months.

How did mothers feel about joining the team? Here is an account from Anthea, a mother who initially had terrific problems with her second child, was involved in supporting her widowed father and sick grandparents, and needed considerable support.

If you feel like a Zombie

If you feel like a Zombie, have been told you are a cabbbage stagnating at home because you have pre-school children, and cannot, or do not want to work – at least until your child is at school, then do what I did, become a rota mum.

My daughter loved nursery and settled down to school very well. I didn't help on the rota then as baby number two was on the way. I eventually took my son to coffee afternoons, and although he spoiled everyone's afternoon because he howled if anyone spoke to him, and clung to me as if stuck to me with that special glue I felt liberated! Many days the only people I saw were the bread man or the milk man and the Nursery staff when I took my daughter. Many of the staff became friends and many of the mums in the Parents Room too. It is good to be able to talk problems over with anyone who will listen and advise and to know you are not alone with your ups and downs.

Later the great day came and my son started Nursery. A different kettle of fish to my daughter, he was difficult to settle in, and I had to stay every morning for a couple of months. After he had settled, I thought my days would be great, the things I could get done would be amazing, but I'd forgotten I still had to ferry both children to school and Nursery, and this totally disrupts your day! So I became a rota Mum!! One morning a week I stay and help staff and I really enjoy it, even though some mornings I need earplugs! I do anything and everything, from playing or reading to the children, or the mundane cutting paper (they get through reams of the stuff) or filling paint pots. Once you have observed just what your children can do, it's amazing how much more tolerant you become at home. I never let my daughter play with plasticine or paint, but my son does both. You should see the enjoyment the children get from painting. That picture you throw away as soon as you get home may have taken your child a long time and is caringly done, often with a detailed commentary of what it is. Remember therefore it is not just a splurge! I love it when a child accepts me as part of the furniture. I've helped for almost two years now and even the shy ones will sometimes ask me to untie a shoelace or button a coat, an honour indeed!

My son totally ignores me while I'm there, it's bliss. It's my morning of the week, I feel needed, useful, and not at all cabbage like! The only way to see just how many ways the staff help *your* child is to do what I do, stay, help, and observe, and maybe learn a little too!

This article was written by a very charming mother living in a comfortable bungalow, with an employed husband and two children. She had elderly parents nearby and helped in their home and regularly had them staying with her – a successful family by most standards. Yet when one looks closely at her article it reveals hidden depths for many housewives and young mothers. *Who had told her she was a cabbage stagnating at home because she had pre-school children?* The first part of this chapter considers how the Centre was trying to meet young mothers needs regardless of class and social situation. Unfortunately many messages are transmitted to women by the media and by the community at large which say that staying at home with pre-schoolers is not very rewarding and is bound to reduce their capacity for intellectual conversation and pursuits. Conversely many others assume they have to be invited to 'help' at nursery and school. However if all is going well they cannot see the point of their help and often feel anxious about getting in the way. We need to change our approach about 'helping' in school. We should consider the need for parents to observe, work with specific activities and with specific children, and bring in their particular strengths to enhance the educational experiences of the children. Social activities such as the coffee afternoon provided occasions for families and very young children to meet together, enjoy each others' company and care about each other. Some parents never make the enormous step of joining a group. It is too threatening and often reinforced inadequacy and anxiety. Yet for Anthea the Centre's two coffee sessions for parents in the Parents Room and playcourt, resulted in her keeping her sanity and not rejoicing her son who was very demanding. It also offered other mothers a chance to share their skills and knowledge and their patience to support a friend ('. . . there but for the grace of God . . .').

The effects of home isolation and psychiatric disturbance were well documented by George Brown and his colleagues in the 1970s. The need to re-create social networks in urban communities for women with young children was a challenge accepted and debated at great length at the Centre. The support of parents by the staff was a new phenomena for some young members and required sensitive help from those with more experience.

'Settling the second child proved to be a very different experience'. So often we encourage parents to leave their child at the earliest possible moment so that the professional can get on with the job. We often forget or are totally unaware of the parental, particularly maternal conflict and feelings of rejection and inadequacy when a child leaves home to join the outside world or nursery, playgroup or school. This mother was grateful for the support and time to help her child gain independence happily and confidently. Each child is so different and should never be labelled difficult or odd or strange because of

their differing stage of maturity and growth – particularly following a confident sibling.

'*And so I became a Rota Mum*' The playgroup movement prides itself on parents taking responsibility regularly on rotas, yet this can be inhibiting for parents unable to cope with this expectation. For some parents the chance to get out of the house each week to 'do' something is very welcome. I suspect that many parents fall into a pattern of involvement by a series of incidents which suggest that it might be nice, helpful, and useful to themselves rather than a planned desire to act as a regular helper committed to a routine at the school or nursery.

The implications of Anthea's description of her involvement were vital for the staff to grasp. This young mother's understanding of the nursery curriculum was enhanced and clarified by her observation and involvement with children and chores. Play is so often under-valued by families. Yet regularly being involved in play with the nursery staff and the children does enrich family life by a better understanding of children's needs and development

> It is very humbling to note her comments on feeling needed and useful and not being cabbage like.

Motherhood has taken quite a knock during the last decade or two. We felt that opening up the Centre in many ways to parents could reduce any negatives particularly the feeling of being unworthy and useless to society opening new doors to positive experiences – educational, social and recreational – it might take the form of classroom involvement or it might be a group experience with other parents. In some cases it could offer an introduction to new training opportunities. In fact two mothers later applied for places on the local Nursery Nurse course.

Intensive involvement with parents with special needs developed in a haphazard and fascinating way. In the early years we worked by responding to crises and mistakes combined with a direct commitment by the senior staff that it was vital to understand the changing influences and demands on family life. The later and more positive approach was in working together to share the enjoyment and the traumas of bringing up children which could help in preventing children going into care as well as in reducing the factors which were contributing towards educational disadvantage.

The range of involvement was wide, drawing extensively on

staff's willingness to respond to actual individual need. We also had to educate ourselves and understand the vast network of voluntary and statutory agencies outside the Centre with which it could be linked to foster this approach.

Some case studies help in illustrating the approach we began to practice intuitively as well as through intense regular discussion:

Family A – What does a mother of five young children need when her husband is in prison for a few years, but he is placed in confinement in the North East of England? Support is such an extraordinary word. It cannot reveal the extent of emotional and practical help required over a number of years to sustain a relationship between an absent husband and father. It cannot reveal the depths of depression, the grief, the worry, the physical hard work of parenting single handed and maintaining the contact with the distant partner. Of course, the staff responded with immense personal love and care for the children and mother. The social services had requested admission of the four pre-schoolers to relieve the mother and give her time to adjust and cope. Several suicide attempts later we had to offer a more flexible approach to prevent her feeling totally de-mothered and inadequate. During intensive discussion we found that on some days she felt bright and cheerful and could cope. On those day one or two children being at home was desirable. She felt that she could give individual attention to several children on these days. On other days she found the huge demands made on her when all four returned from a full day at the Centre intolerable. So gradually we devised with her involvement and the support of her social worker, a flexible system of attendance for the children. On some days, usually Monday and Friday all four came to the Centre. The mother would joke that it gave her time to prepare for the weekend on her own with all the kids and a day to get over it. On the Tuesday, Wednesday and Thursday we had two or three of the children depending on whom she felt needed more of her attention. As the children all had secure Family Groups with a nursery nurse to extend the consistent handling we had discussed with the mother, this system, on the whole, worked well. The main conflict for staff was maintaining some continuity in the children's educational programme. As most staff had been trained to expect children to attend regularly at nursery, a more flexible pattern of attendance required more flexibility in planning, assessing and evaluating the children's progress.

On days when the mother was particularly low all the children attended the Centre. The mother herself might spend time at the Centre, in the nursery rooms, in the office and in the parents' room with other mothers for company and support. She might stay and have lunch. Her social worker or health visitor might join her. She might prefer to stay at home. One of the staff would pop in to check she was alright and stay and chat. The social worker might be called in to provide more specialised counselling. Several new forms of involvement developed with this family. We supported the mother when she wrote to her M.P. for help in getting her husband transferred to a nearer prison to encourage regular contact with the children. We all shared her awe and amazement when the House of Commons insignia on the envelope provided her with a new hope when the letter inside promised to investigate the situation. We were thrilled when the husband was, in fact, moved to Nottingham prison. The deputy head took her and the children on several occasions to visit and played with some of the children in the visiting room whilst waiting to see their father.

When this mother was exhausted and felt little hope of ever returning to a normal family life, the Head and social worker discussed avenues of relief with a holiday in mind. The mother's extended family lived in the West of England. Although the maternal grandmother was very supportive and spent holidays with her daughter and grandchildren, it was far too expensive to take five children away on holiday. Contact with NACRO, the charity which supports prison offenders and their families, resulted in a cheque to cover the cost of the train fare for the whole family to visit the grandmother. There was great excitement in the Centre before the holiday. The Head drove the family to the station and saw them off safely and we all waited with anticipation for a postcard.

It was this sort of exchange between the family and the staff which enriched job satisfaction and helped the family rebuild its life around the gulf of separation and poverty. The mother was overweight. Some years later she wanted to diet to reduce her size to a voluptuous, attractive size 14 to be instantly desirable on her husband's return. Some staff gallantly went on a diet to encourage her, but when the diet failed they were also available to share here realistic appraisal that a sound sex life should be based on love and a quality relationship not on physical attractiveness.

Family B – When prisoners are confined for 15 years the situation poses even more problems. A very young baby will be growing towards adolescence when father returns. Primary age children will be leaving school. A healthy, normal, attractive woman used to a satisfactory sexual relationship will have had to make painful choices of coping with separation. The single-handed parenting with the stigma of prisoners and low status for many years, reduces the partner at home in self-esteem and produces immense psychological, social and emotional burdens.

Besides the commitment of personal care and attention for the mother by the staff, we wanted with this family to devise a system of contact between the Centre and the husband. The youngest child was only eighteen months old when he began attending the Centre two or three days a week to relieve his mother and to give her an opportunity to travel regularly long distances into the Home Counties to visit her husband. The day before the visit was traumatic and the day after was filled with unhappiness and despair. The staff's listening ear was vital and time during the morning had to be set aside for this.

One approach towards fostering a link with the father was successful. We were developing a Language Project in the Under 3's unit. A speech therapist was devising with the Matron a scheme to foster an enriched vocabulary with the youngest children. Their parent(s) were involved and, in some cases, grandparents. We were improvising a range of simple toys and equipment to encourage more language exchange between the parent and the child. Through the mother in family B we corresponded with the father to find out if he could help with making some of the equipment in his leisure and educational periods. After some negotiation a steady flow of excellently made toys began to arrive after the prison visits. Admiration and pleasure from staff, other parents and the children raised the mother's morale and then her contribution to the youngest child's education. She began to stay and play with the other children as well as her own.

There were many troughs of despair in her first years of separation, of course. Problems with older children resulted in the Matron or Head liaising with the local primary and secondary school and encouraging the mother to share the anxieties with the key staff working with her older children. A need and desire for social outings, not only of prisoners' wives but many other single women resulted in the development of social outings to the pub for a basket meal, to play darts, to go to the theatre. In a community where women do not assert their independence and are not welcomed alone in male dominated leisure facilities, there was a great need to encourage women to organise themselves in supportive groups to go out and enjoy themselves together without male escorts.

Non accidental injury is a distressing phenomena that revolts society. Devising patterns of care and support for the child, the partner witnessing the act and the partner who has hurt the child require, sensitivity, firmness, openness and stamina, emotional and physical. During the early years at the Centre, we accepted the responsibility to work as positively as was possible with a high number of children who had received injuries or were 'at risk' of physical abuse. This focused on working closely with the family and the other key workers in the community.

Some of the strategies resulted in an intense input for a short period with no further injuries to the children and a change in situations which reduced the expectation that they might arise again. Others required regular sustained support for the parents, careful diagnostic skills in identifying the child's needs and close supervision of the staff dealing with the day-to-day situation. It required strong leadership at the Centre. As none of the four senior staff had any social work training it was a compliment to them how much faith the local work team, paediatric assessment unit, health visitor team and NSPCC Inspector had in the Centre. We devised various channels of communication, regular assessment meetings and shoulders to lean on when we felt that we were making little progress. An example of an approach to this aspect of involvement can be demonstrated by Family C.

Family C – Here was an unusual situation as we had to develop new techniques. A father was left with four children, one of 18 months who was very tragically hurt by the mother's cohabitee. The injured child required surgery and intensive hospital treatment which was then linked to day care supervision and help. The approaches for this young father were extraordinary and could only be offered because of a high child/staff ratio, and extra staff with no daily child contact responsibility.

Again the development of listening skills was crucial. The father needed hours of time to talk, reflect, pour out his anger and hurt and grief. He needed time to adjust to his changed status and new role. Having given up work to look after the children he had to learn all the childcare and home-making skills quickly. He needed advice with cooking, washing different fabrics, shopping cheaply and generally, surviving on Social Security. He had never been unemployed and the financial adjustment was enormous. His loss of independence and esteem in the community was shattering. His loss of daily contact with other men was bewildering. Our role varied from mothering him to helping him 'mother' his children. He needed praise and encouragement in tackling the new survival skills, he also needed firm, consistent friendship which not only nurtured him but gently pushed him onwards to independence. We accepted the early years of dependence on the nursery and the staff but always worked towards him rebuilding his life and returning to his own self-reliance and strengths.

He stumbled through a variety of depressive states including for a short time dependence on drugs and alcohol to face everyday life. His daily appearance in the nursery varied in intensity. Everyday there was discussion on the progress of his child. There was delayed development, physically and intellectually. Temper tantrums and toileting problems were consistent for several years requiring great patience, skill and affection from the staff and father. The input of the social worker, health visitor and psychiatric staff from the local clinic reinforced and strengthened staff morale and taught us many ways of working with them consistently to help this parent. His daily coffee was made with much affectionate leg pulling, changing him gradually from a dependent client to a cheerful parent who would make coffee for everyone.

He was involved in much planning to help his child overcome some of her developmental handicaps. His anxiety regarding special school provision at 5 years required much honest exchange to help him face up to the possibility. Different staff contributed in different ways. The Deputy Matron had an especially close relationship. She often lent him her car and gave him errands to do or he used it for hospital appointments. The Deputy Head took the older children camping in the school holidays with an organisation she was involved in. The family group nursery nurse gave everybody help with a growing 3–5 year old. The nursery teacher developed finer skills of assessment of intellectual delay and sound record keeping and devised specific play activities.

The Head and Matron kept the links between the specialists' help open and carried the responsibility of observing staff, counselling them, praising them and sometimes relieving them of the pressure by drawing the father into the office for discussion and comfort.

Many of our contacts with families referred by Social Services required this 'learning by doing' process matched with assessing and adjusting continually following observation, discussion or even unexpected and renewed crisis. We accepted children whose parents were agoraphobic, epileptic, schizophrenic, mentally and physically handicapped, violent, timid and inexperienced, depressive and suicidal. Some parents had rejected the child following poor bonding at birth due to hospital routines or childbirth difficulties. Thus the range of approaches and techniques had to vary and be flexible for individual cases.

Alongside this daily work with the children and parents needing individual attention, there were parents being involved incidentally and regularly in the classrooms, playcourt and parents room. The staff were beginning to come to terms with the wider range of demands being made on them which did not match their original expectation or training for the job.

In many instances of parental involvement in schools, staff are quite happy if the parent is involved in a spare room, a corridor or the hall. To involve them actively in the classroom presented conflict, new challenges, raised anxieties and sometimes fostered a feeling of being devalued professionally.

A working party of staff spent some weeks devising a policy document of aims for parental involvement. We felt it would be helpful to share common aims, using a consistent approach throughout the centre. This document was then discussed by the whole staff and adapted until it was felt that the patterns of involvement were broad enough to meet the wide ranging needs of the families using the Centre and could be met by the varying skills and expertise at the Centre. First there was a need to consider staff attitudes and clarify the changing skills required by staff to work closely with individual parents – mothers and fathers although inevitably it was usually with mothers. A particular problem or perhaps strength for the staff was the fact that all staff, including the caretaker, were women. Some had experienced marital difficulties, many had survived and enjoyed parenting. Several had recently understood the reality of a partner made redundant. Others were very young and still acquiring life skills.

It was a real challenge to be impartial and non-judgemental and required maturity, and a great deal of love combined with personal support to talk through new situations and crises involving staff with parents more closely.

The Centre's policy towards parental involvement

In the early years there was some resistance to the breadth of the involvement which could de-skill the professional nursery worker. There was often a genuine fear and anxiety of parent domination, interference and personality clashes mixed with an anxiety of intervening between the parent and child, which might undermine parental or staff authority. Staff had excellent relationships with young children, but limited experience of coping with adults and sometimes poorly developed skills in adult relationships. Some staff felt that their training and vocation was exclusively to work with the children and that their professionalism was at risk if shared with parents. One has to acknowledge the concern for limited facilities in the classroom for extra adults and siblings, and to recognise the need for imagination and thought in planning to accommodate the respective needs of children, the parents and the staff.

Many parents had a genuine fear and anxiety of the trained professional; the 'expert' and the mystique often reinforced feelings of inadequacy. Some parents lived a long way from the Centre and the children were transported by taxi each day. Staff therefore only saw these parents occasionally. Some parents were at work all day. Opportunities for discussion and participation were then limited. Many families had other obligations which prevented daily participation in Centre events. There was the husband's shift, care of elderly relatives, a large family, poor health, a new baby. We must acknowledge the feeling of initial apathy towards any close involvement between staff and parents when there were enormous social problems. There were also a minority of families who took advantage of the system and the staff interest, to manipulate it for their own ends.

Acknowledging the problems of developing close links between the staff and parents was balanced by our clear aims of why and how it is essential to develop sound trusting links with the families using the Centre

Over a period of years our aims became :–

1 To establish a working relationship between the family and the staff.
2 To foster confidence and communication between the family and the staff.
3 To share information and knowledge between the family and the staff.
4 To draw on the resources of the family and the Centre in order to develop the child to its full potential.
5 To achieve a deeper understanding of patterns of family life.

It was important to express the aims in terms of daily experience which then had meaning for the least experienced staff as well as helped the most entrenched and insecure staff move towards involvement.

1 *To establish a working relationship between staff and families*

This was achieved as staff began to understand the major influences on the child's early years, which occurred when staff encouraged parents to take an active part in their child's education. There had to be a genuine interest in the whole family. Staff were to offer a warm welcome when parents delivered their children making opportunities for listening to needs and problems, with sympathetic discussion. It was essential that the nursery was an inviting, comfortable place for parents in the classroom, to promote confidence and ease in the busy nursery. Seating for parents endorsed the explicit welcome and expectation to come into the playroom at any time.

Home visiting established the initial links with the family and was followed up after enrolment at the Centre when absence and poor take-up of the facilities became evident. The Head or Matron initially visited families when a place was available at the Centre. The Centre brochure was prepared with the name of the child and the staff responsible for his/her care and education. The Head or Matron were able to answer questions as well as ask about individual need. Flexibility was discussed, for example a full-time place could be offered which could include up to three meals each day. Ordinary part-time places commonly offered in the nursery schools could be extended with a meal and holiday place to support some families. The first home visit established the welcome and interest of Centre staff and explained the facilities for both child and adult at the Centre. The teacher then followed up this visit with more explanation of the classroom organisation, endorsing the needs and expectation of close opportunity for exchange of ideas, problems and interests. The child met his/her teacher and observed the parent and newcomer relating and was encouraged to participate in this early contact. This visit was followed by an invitation to attend a coffee session in the next week to meet the Family Group nursery nurse, other new children and parents and to be introduced to the busy routine at the Centre. This was an important time for all staff in the team to demonstrate their interest and genuine welcome.

2 *To foster confidence and communication between the family and staff*

The initial visits prepared the parent for our expectation that the settling in of their child was very important and should not be rushed. It was crucial to future relationships that time was taken to introduce young children gradually to a new routine, strange adults, different expectations and new peer group relationships. This was an invaluable time for helping parents understand their children's own individual needs. It was an excellent time for establishing a friendship and understanding that together the staff and parents were going to work towards supporting each other and sharing skills and expertise. We therefore expected all families to spend at least a week and more if needed to begin this transition from home to school routine.

These mini–visits were very interesting. Some parents coped with the new routine very ably; asking questions; playing with their child at new activities; moving about the room with confidence. Others showed anxiety, indifference, embarrassment and occasionally impatience and hostility. Others were relieved that the break from home could be gradual, giving time to the parent as well as the child to adjust to new influences on their relationships. It became obvious that the new skills required of the nursery staff were much more complex if they were to work with the parent as well as the child at this delicate time. The mini-visits were staggered so that the nursery nurse and the teacher were available to welcome and settle the new arrivals whilst the rest of the team were able to concentrate on the regular routine, relieving their colleagues to give their time to the family.

During the mini-visits children who were to have meals were gently introduced to these with their parents joining in. A mother and child might join us for breakfast or lunch several times before the admission of the child. This enabled them to observe our routines and expectations of table manners and social skills. There was discussion about feeding habits and routines, favourite foods and independence at a family meal occasion.

These mini-visits were then followed by daily contact with the family to enable the initial relationship to grow and improve so that communication could develop easily. Coffee mornings, newsletters and parents' meetings increased the exchange of confidence and involvement. We did, above all, value the daily regular informal contact with the family when arriving or collecting children. It was very noticeable that the few families we had least contact with were those who were not in easy prampushing distance of the Centre and were transported by Education or Social Services transport.

3 *To share information and knowledge between family and staff*

The resources and methods used to promote this exchange were organised in four areas:

1. The nursery rooms
2. The parents' room
3. Parents' meetings
4. Home visits

THE NURSERY ROOMS

The nursery environment could no longer be considered entirely organised for the children's needs. Through our experience it became evident that it was essential to design playrooms with ample adult facilities which automatically offered parents evidence that the nursery was a place for them. We improvised parents' areas in all rooms in the Centre. Armchairs, notice boards, and coffee tables were prominently placed and every effort made to encourage and involve the family in the child's environment.

A great deal of information was shared informally in the parents' area by a member of staff having a coffee with a parent. Signals were picked up by staff of parents under stress or anxious as they delivered or collected children. A quick exchange of concern resulted in withdrawal to a private place for confidential discussion when necessary.

We also worked towards an exchange of verbal, and written communication, and participation in the Centre. The newsletter, has been mentioned earlier (see page 124). Parents were invited to join the team on a regular weekly basis for a session and help in the nursery. They were not selected in any way.

THE PARENTS' ROOM

This was a tiny rather claustrophobic room at the back of the Centre next to the Head's room and opposite the staff room.

There were armchairs and tables, noticeboards, a sink with tea and coffee making ingredients on the draining board, and toys for children and magazines.

Any parent could use the room at any time to sit and relax in. This was a good time to meet, or make friends. Staff could introduce shy parents into the room or join parents for a chat.

Booklets and pamphlets from Health Education Council and Department of Health and Social Security, were displayed and available. Articles from magazines cut out and pinned to noticeboards, educational magazines such as Early Childhood were left on the coffee tables.

Workshops and meetings were arranged in consultation with parents. Speakers, demonstrations, films and special groups were organised each term with a mix of and exchange of ideas and counselling and social relaxation.

For example:
(a) A counselling group met for ten weeks each Wednesday with a Marriage Guidance Counsellor to talk about children, family and personal difficulties. This group was organised by the Head for women with a wide range of problems and who needed a regular outlet for discussion with a skilled counsellor in a self-help group.

(b) Parents were invited to see a puppet show with their children in the Playcourt and then join the puppeteers in the Parents' Room and Staff Room to make simple puppets and talk about using them at home with the children.

(c) The Area Health Education Counsellor called to introduce herself and gave a film catalogue of topics useful for parents' meetings. She was invited to join the parents to show a film on common accidents in the home and lead a discussion on prevention.

(d) Creative workshops were organised using staff and people from the community with particular skills. An elderly lady living nearby was skilled at knitting and crochet. An interest in crochet was voiced by some mums so we invited the neighbour to share her skill and knowledge in a workshop. We could not pay her but she did not mind. The mothers bought a plant pot to demonstrate their pleasure.

A nursery nurse was very gifted with flower arranging. The Deputy Head enjoyed macrame and the Head made her own earrings. These hobbies were offered as workshops for mothers to give them an enjoyable creative afternoon with pleasant company. Two mothers were so interested in the earring making that they opened a stall on the market for a few weeks and sold many which they made at home following the workshop.

A mother and toddler group used the playcourt next to the parents' room each Tuesday and Thursday. This was an excellent opportunity to share ideas on children's play and development. A member of staff supervised the children with a rota of the mothers. They informally shared children's behaviour problems, discipline, interests, activities and together became involved in the play.

A young teacher set up a toy library and when she left two nursery nurses ran it. Equipment was bought from fund raising schemes and lent to families free of charge. This offered another opportunity for staff to guide and discuss the toys and for parents to question and search for new ideas to stimulate their children's interest. One of the mothers organised a book stall each year and good, cheap, paperbacks were on sale for families – in a town with no bookshop.

PARENTS' MEETINGS

During the early years, many parents' evenings were of a social nature. We had little confidcence in our ability to interest parents in the education of their children outside nursery hours. The social occasions were, Barn Dances, Beetle Drives, Bonfire Party and Darts Matches.

Gradually we began tentatively to change direction at least once or twice a year in parent meetings. We used film and video as a successful stimulant to parental interest in understanding the life of the Centre. General 8mm films of nursery activities produced over-subscribed film showings as all the family, including grandma and auntie wanted to see the child on film.

Our most successful Parents' Evenings were three meetings organised by each team for their parents. A video film specially constructed with the help of the Teachers' Centre Warden was shown to demonstrate the learning opportunities in the Centre.

Each team made a film of their approach to their work. it demonstrated the following aspects of nursery work:

(a) free creative play, chosen by the child at any time.

(b) group activities organised by the nursery nurse for the Family Group each session.

(c) directed play for groups or individuals, eg. large construction building ring and singing games a special activity in the water trolley eg. with magnets, or coloured inks.

(d) the teacher working with individual children assessing their understanding on a certain topic, or working on a specifically designed language programme.

(e) Parent participation informally in the classroom.

(f) Parents preparing for and working on the regular rota.

These video films were accompanied by a crêche for families who could not get babysitters and a cheese and wine buffet to enjoy whilst discussing the film. We were delighted to find that more than sixty families were represented at these evenings, some coming to two evenings as they had children in different nursery rooms.

Another type of successful Parents' Evening was achieved with a practical demonstration of early mathematics learning. Parents came to handle and 'play' with the equipment and discuss how children acquired the concepts and language of number, size and shape. There was no lecture, no film. The whole Centre was set up for a normal day's activity at 7.30 pm and parents were encouraged to involve themselves with paint, clay, blocks, water, sand and so on. Members of staff were at each activity to lead the discussion and answer questions. Books and apparatus and toys were on sale from a good Nottingham toyshop so that dominoes, lottos and jigsaws could be purchased to reinforce the enjoyable and enlightening evening had by all.

4 *To draw on the resources of family and Centre in order to develop children to their full potential*

Having established rapport with families staff continued to develop the above methods to fulfil this fourth aim. We extended by developing trusting, confident relationships with our other colleagues in the community. During the early years our colleagues in the Social Work team and health visitor team became an extension of the nursery team. Regular telephone, written communication and visiting produced a sound trust between three disciplines, all of whom worked with the same family. There was an exchange of advice and information on the family needs; there were regular requests for guidance, exchanges of ideas, offers of new approaches to the support of the child and family as well as developing an understanding for the changing needs of the staff. Together and with consultation we worked towards an improved service for families with young children to ensure that the health and education of these children was the best that could be acquired within the constraints of the services. Similarly where social work intervention was required we supported the family to help them overcome or come to terms with their limitations.

The Health Visitors and Social Workers visited regularly and talked to the staff and parents informally in the classrooms, or withdrew to the office for private discussion. One Social Worker worked regularly with us each Wednesday morning, learning about young children's needs, our staff dynamics and being available for consultation with parents. Together we were able to initiate new practice to meet the challenges presented by families or very occasionally comfort each other that all the combined effort with the parents had not met the needs of the child and the child was to go into daycare or be adopted.

We were very pleased to enjoy a good relationship with the local paediatric assessment unit (P.A.U.). Children and parents were referred to the Centre for our continued assessment and diagnosis of educational and developmental delay and handicap. We were able to refer children to the P.A.U. through our good contacts with the General Practitioner, Health Visitor and School Nurse. Case conferences were usually lengthy and informative, often with the Centre fulfilling an important role as having the most regular ongoing contact with the child and family under review. Such interprofessional liaison was further extended by enjoying the services of the local speech therapist. The Matron working with the youngest children devised a language programme with the help of the speech therapist to promote and foster language skills with the support and involvement of the family. The children's language skills had been assessed by the Matron and the Speech Therapist. A realistic programme in the Baby Den had been devised to concentrate on development of language and the family, sometimes the mother sometimes the grandmother had been involved in the programme so that they could continue the work at home each week. This was a positive approach to the children's needs in the Baby Den rather than a remedial approach with compensatory intervention.

The teaching staff referred children to the speech therapist, and the speech therapist referred children to the Centre. Together they assessed and planned individual children's language and speech needs to compensate for retardation, slow development, physical and medical difficulties. Time was given to these children for individual help in the busy routine of a nursery session. The parent was often attending the therapy sessions at the Health Centre and at the nursery as well. So once again the sharing of skills between colleagues and the family offered the child a better chance to reach his/her full potential.

A new psychologist joined the School Psychological service. We approached him to meet us to consider ways of preventing serious developmental delay and overcoming handicap difficulties by working very closely with the staff at the Centre and the families in the community.

Having established good relaionships between staff and parents, and shared much information and expertise, we felt an important area for promoting the continuity of the early learning experiences at the Centre and in the home, was to encourage parents to continue their interest and involvement in the primary school. The nursery teachers met the parents of children about to leave the Centre for school to discuss the child's development, achievements, potential and difficulties if any. They were informed of their child's intellectual and social ability and progress and urged to follow this through with the infant staff. Meetings were then held with the local infant departments to continue this exchange of information and sharing of expertise and knowledge which should foster the continuity for child and parent at transition into school.

5 *To achieve a deeper understanding of patterns of family life*

We felt strongly that to separate the important influences of the family on the child from the newer stranger influences of Centre life was harmful to the changing patterns of educating and caring for young children. It was essential to see the two differing worlds overlap, complement, and supplement each other. This could only be achieved by trust, friendship, information, discussion and appreciation of each other. The lives of many of our young children were very complex, making enormous demands on them. An increasing number of families did not enjoy a settled, organised and happy routine. Pressures on families with young children were changing in relation to unemployment, poverty in an apparently affluent society, marital breakdown and poor housing. It was important to know local community mores and values. Poor attendance at Parent Evenings need not be from indifference and apathy. It could be the result of difficult shifts, no babysitters, mothers employed on twilight shifts in the factory and so on. Therefore staff with a genuine desire to work closely with families to help them understand their children's needs had to understand the families and be adaptable, flexible, non-judgemental and caring and understanding. If the Centre was to be used by families it had to meet these families' needs.

Thus it became accepted that the Centre was available to meet a range of family needs. It was accepted that staff needed to develop new skills in communication and consultation with families and other colleagues. There were, of course, tremendous difficulties and stressful confrontations in our attempt to achieve this. The Parents' Room and Mother and Toddler Group survived many changes in direction. Staff and parent goodwill was often exploited. Yet each time the good intentions of a new development suffered difficulties it was exciting to reflect later on the patience, re-assessment, re-organisation and renewed enthusiasm and tackle and overcome the difficulties to make it work.

There were periods of development when users took responsibility and control, sharing in decision making and organisation. At other times as experienced parents moved on with their children into the primary phase, or during family and community tensions such as strikes and redundancies, parents own needs took precedence. This might take the form of neglecting to supervise and care for the children in the group whilst adult discussion took place. Failure to share in clearing up toys, coffee cups and cigarette ends produced anger and conflict between staff and parent and parent and parent. Money went missing, equipment disappeared, participants lost confidence in the group.

It became very clear that a community worker based in the Parents Room could offer support, continuity and advice to sustain the range of activities offered or organised by the users. Thus began a campaign to create a new post in the Centre to work particularly with adults rather than children.

CHAPTER 8

The Centre as a community resource

One of the deepest conflicts for nursery staff is between the amount of attention they can give to the children in their care when they are expected to also take an interest in their family. As the Centre began to increase its involvement with the community this conflict of priorities sharpened. Some staff withdrew from active participation in other Centre activities. Others recognised the needs and encouraged and supported some initiatives and came to terms with the dilemma. A few became engrossed in the possibilities and worked increasingly to support the wider dimension of nursery work.

It was vital to help staff appreciate that their expertise and skills would enrich other Centre initiatives, not de-skill them and make them redundant. It was necessary to reassure them that the extra work with students, comprehensive pupils and YOP trainees offered new positive perspectives for these young people. We all knew the lack of facilities in the town for families and young children whether for meetings or socials or clubs. Time was required to consider the value of sharing our resources at the Centre with the community, many of whom were our parents or were working with young children.

The joint DES/DHSS Circular (1978) Coordination of Services for Under fives had urged local authorities co-ordinating services for the under fives to maximise the use of existing resources. We took it literally and began to open the Centre for all sorts of community involvement. We had no extra staff to develop this work, we once more stumbled along agreeing to support this initiative or creating the climate and space to establish that one. It just grew and grew. Sometimes the atmosphere was chaotic; too noisy, too many bodies, too much mess, too many demands. Staff became irritable and tired. The caretaker had frequent tantrums. At other times things flowered, improved and demonstrated a mature response by the outsiders and the staff working together and sorting out problems. It was essential that staff had confidence and opportunities to talk with the senior staff to express the conflict they felt with developments. It was vital that the senior staff protected and cushioned colleagues during periods of tension and overwork and absorbed some of the conflict in their roles.

The Centre as a social meeting place

Colleagues visiting the Centre who were interested in parent involvement would sigh with envy that we had a designated Parents' Room. Even though it was small, inadequately designed and furnished, it was a room which parents could call their own with a door to close on the noise and bustle of the nursery, providing a refuge and a common meeting place.

Tea and coffee were always available and smoking was permitted. Consumables extended to a glass of wine and sherry and cream cakes at the various 'fuddles' (Fuddle – Nottinghamshire term for a party, a social gathering). to celebrate birthdays and Christmas, a pregnancy or relief that one was not pregnant after all. Groups of mothers would meet after settling their children in the playrooms, for a good gossip. Women, toddlers, babies, prams and shopping bags were crammed into this room which resounded with laughter, gossip, children crying and chinking crockery. Other parents came later after shopping and would relax there before collecting children to take home. These sessions were informal and unsupervised by staff. Occasionally staff popped in for a chat or brought a new parent in to be made welcome.

In the Parents' Room there was a second-hand rail of adult and children's clothes, books, literature on child health and toys, posters, information on societies, eg., Parents Anonymous, notices about Toddler groups and the Toy Library. This was a place for women to meet on neutral ground, to get them out of the isolation of their homes, to help them create new friendships and a network of support outside the extended nuclear family.

Some staff were fascinated that a large number of these mothers virtually lived in the Parents' Room and rarely invited each other to their homes. Other staff resented their use of the room and frequently expressed their opinion that the women would be better employed at home, cleaning and cooking and home making, as they had done when they were young and newly married. It became necessary to encourage staff to join parents for a coffee occasionally to help them understand the women and observe their enjoyment.

The informal use of the room was extended by organising a coffee morning and a coffee afternoon each week for a wider range of parents to enjoy a session which might include a visiting speaker or a demonstration or exhibition especially arranged for them. A part-time teacher joined the two nursery teams on alternate weeks to release the class teachers to hostess these sessions. The Head and Matron looked after the crêche in the Playcourt. During the process of establishing the Group and Toy Library it was essential to involve staff in some of the work. It was therefore necessary for the Head and Matron to be flexible to fill in any crucial gaps with the care of toddlers or nursery children. The bad days were of course, the wet, rainy days which resulted in 60 nursery children and anything up to 25 toddlers having to stay indoors, in rather cramped conditions. Also all went well when all staff were present. When flu, sickness and diarrhoea, family problems and staggered holidays clashed reducing the staff numbers drastically, tensions increased, tempers shortened and the conflict was clear. These difficult patches had to be discussed and shared and approaches adapted. Thus gradually emerged the Mother/Toddler Group, the Toy Library and a regular set of activities for the mothers. Fathers were encouraged to join these activities but rarely did. It was truly a female dominated world.

The weekly meetings were extended to a monthly parents' social which included Beetle Drives with Fish and Chip Suppers, Darts Matches at the local Inn, Toy Exhibitions, Folk Singing Night with Buffet, Barn Dances and so on. For many single parents they were the only social occasion to look forward to. Most of our socials did not require a male escort, and women began to gain confidence in developing the range of their nights out. In the Baby Den most of the

families were on a very restricted income. The Baby Den staff agreed
to collect 50p a week from the mothers towards a night out together
every few months. This offered a new dimension in relationships for
the mothers and for the staff. Ten or fifteen women by now, all on
Christian name terms could enjoy each others company at the local
Inn or Restaurant. The women began to appreciate each others
interests and strengths. Conversation ranged across the children, the
family, school and problems and was liberally spattered with much
laughter and leg pulling. Tired withdrawn mothers began to blos-
som, others became leaders in the group – often a very new experience.

All the staff in this small group were married with their own children. It is a great compliment to their families how much they shared
their mothers and wives with her work colleagues and clients. At
parties dances and fund raising it was very reassuring to see staff husbands, boyfriends and children enjoying the fun with the Centre
families and communities.

We were very fortunate to have easy access to a number of
minibuses and other transport. There were S.S.D. and Education
minibuses, Leisure Services and Youth Service vehicles. Primary
and secondary schools had their own transport nearby to our Centre.
A community coach based at Sutton Centre was also used. Many
staff could drive and we paid for minibus tests to increase the independence of teachers and family group nursery nurses. They could
arrange to take families and children out at any time during the day
as well as plan outings at the weekends. Outings included the simple
nearby visit to parks, garden centres, farms, the town of Mansfield
or Nottingham. Further afield the children had first hand experience
of the airport, the canal, the railway station, the zoo and the Peak
District. Parents were always involved in these visits and the demand
increased for outings to Alton Towers, to London and to the Seaside.

Social meetings for specific groups were needed and the Centre
was made available. The Gingerbread group established itself
using the parents' room weekly as a base. A club for parents with
mentally handicapped children and adults was welcome each
month. The Childminders Support Group used the facilities every
fortnight. Their key workers, usually social workers, were present
thus relieving the nursery staff of any responsibility, other than
to welcome them and share the resources – furniture, crockery,
and toys.

Preparing for an outing

Family Group outing

Clubs and Classes

Through the years a number of clubs and classes were arranged or developed. Some became established by a key community worker, others following requests by parents for a particular event.

A slimming club became a thriving enterprise for a short while. This was organised by the school nurse. Obesity and overweight were prevalent in Kirkby due to poor diet, little exercise and, in some cases, comfort eating. The school nurse worked in the next door special school for mentally handicapped children. Besides encouraging the mothers with diet problems, she gradually introduced some of the adolescent handicapped children into the club. They were accepted into the group and mothers took a great deal of interest in them.

A well-women health day drew in many other colleagues in the community to run workshops and enrich exhibitions. Parents were invited to workshops on Family Planning, Eating for Good Health, Stress in Modern Living, and coping with Depression. Exhibitions included giving up smoking, alcohol and drug abuse, many child health aspects and support groups such as Parents Anonymous and Alcoholics Anonymous.

The East Midlands Arts Council was approached with requests to finance some community enterprises. They were very helpful and provided workshops on music, puppet making and a performance by a small travelling theatre group.

Workshops on Play were popular. The Matron, Head, Deputy and a classroom teacher from time to time offered practical workshops on playing with young children. Some were open to all parents, eg. 'Things to do on a rainy day at home'. Othere were for groups of mothers committing themselves to regular weekly help in the nursery. These workshops were designed to help them become more aware of the value of the play activities and their role in getting involved in it with the children.

Colleagues in the Health Department and in Health Education offered films, workshops and videos on many relevant aspects of childcare and family health.

We knew there was a need for and an interest in adult education classes. Yet many of our families could not afford a term's fee to enrol. Others had little confidence to enter the local comprehensive school. A few had no experience of committing themselves to a certain number of weekly meetings. We approached the F.E. Adult Education tutor for help with this dilemma. We wanted 'Play as You Learn' Classes and some outreach work done in the Nursery Centre to build up the parents confidence in this new area of education for themselves. A very successful experiment came after an approach to the W.E.A. The W.E.A. Women's Studies Group agreed to do some investigation meetings to identify some common ground for a women's course. It was a challenge for the tutor as her main experience in tutoring was with middle class women using the W.E.A. classes. She had to adapt her techniques and work towards increasing the mothers' skills in group work and sharing ideas. The result of the outreach work was a very interesting 8 week course for women which covered family dynamics, stress, children and marital problems, civil rights and welfare rights. It began a new dimension in the Centre of continuing education for adults whilst their children enjoyed their pre-school education.

Support and Supervision

Colleagues in other agencies, statutory and voluntary valued the support we could offer to families with whom they had close contact.

The number of children with special needs was high. The range of parents with special needs was even higher. Therefore the move towards a more flexible approach to working with the child and the family was essential. Several parents were severely handicapped with debilitating diseases, confined to wheelchairs and mobility aids. Their children were able bodied, bright and happy, developing in a very satisfying way. The parents could rarely visit the Centre as transport was essential. It was good that the Centre was close by. Staff could walk to their homes and talk to them about their children's progress. The Matron and Head would collect the parents and wheelchair and give them a happy few hours involvement with their own child and others. This was infrequent due to other ill health problems, tiredness and exposure to colds etc! Yet it offered comfort to the parent and gave the child a wonderful opportunity to share the parent with other children.

Parents and other adults identified as 'at risk' through depression were sometimes introduced to our facilities and encouraged to join our social events. Psychiatric workers were appreciative of the positive effects this involvement had on patients who were rehabilitated back into the community, yet needed gentle encouragement. One old lady in particular was able to put her occupational therapy to good use. She enjoyed sitting in an armchair watching children and sewing beautiful soft toys for use in nursery as well as for stalls at our fund raising events.

Access to children under our supervision was thankfully only required rarely. This produced mixed feelings amongst staff. It was difficult not to take sides with parents separated or divorced who poured out their problems, animosity and anger. Where one parent had custody and the other was not considered responsible for unsupervised access, the local social work office was the usual meeting place for parent and child. On several occasions following tense and sometimes angry consultations with both parents we agreed with the social work request to supervise the weekly and fortnightly parental visit.

Family A provided too much conflict for staff to accommodate either parent. We had been involved in case conferences on adult physical violence, child neglect and strategies to keep the child out of care. When the mother failed to gain custody of her child many staff reasonably felt maternal distress and anger, as women usually, are given a very young child's care and they felt it was wrong that the father should be successful. As staff felt so concerned with their own attitudes towards the family it was agreed that the Head and Deputy Head would share the supervision. The situation stretched everyone's patience to the limit. The Head's office or Parents' Room were available often for some privacy but to no avail. The family tensions, and the mother's unpredictability led to a gradual breakdown in regular visiting. Yet the visiting was invaluable to the child who missed his mother and we felt in the long term it had been right to offer some support.

Family B – the father wanted to see his three children who attended the Centre. As he worked shifts we had to be very flexible. One week he joined us to play with the children mid-morning. He had coffee whilst the children had their milk and fruit. We tried to offer some privacy to enjoy his children, yet often he was involved with other children too. The following week his shift changed. As his children stayed for tea he joined us at his own table with the children whilst we gave tea to the others nearby.

In both cases the other parent who had custody was dismayed and angry by our attempt to be impartial and co-operate with both parents for the sake of their child's right to know them. It was a challenge for staff, yet the strength of commitment combined with personal support from the senior staff and opportunities to discuss these conflicts helped the staff understand the breadth of family need which could be strengthened by the support of the Centre.

Training

Our links with secondary schools, colleges, training units in the hospitals, MSC schemes and other establishments produced regular requests for training and work experience at the Centre.

Courses on Preparation for Parenthood and Childcare, community experience and pre-training practical experience were vital parts of our training support network. We endeavoured to share our approach and learning with young adolescents, students of all types throughout the many agencies who care and educate young children.

At first it was a steady trickle of requests for visits and observations. We very quickly had to adjust our goodwill to a more reasonable commitment. We felt that social work, health visitor, midwife, teacher and nursery nurse support was essential. Some of these colleagues were placed with us for a block period, others for weekly visits. We restricted our secondary pupils to the nearby school as these children were those likely to be our parents of the future. We wanted them to know the Centre well as a place to go for advice, social and recreational contact for themselves, as well as nursery experience for their children. We insisted on at least six weekly sessions for them to gain an insight into our work and for us to establish a warm relationship with them.

We felt it was important to talk with students if possible before their placements. We regularly gave talks, organised workshops, showed video films of our work and spent time with the teachers and lecturers too, to give an insight into the dimension of work to be experienced at the Centre. One of the benefits of this approach was that we gradually shared the training opportunities with the staff.

The Head, Matron and the two deputies all undertook regular lecturing and workshops. Nursery teachers and nursery nurses were taken along to give their view of the work. This partnership was particularly exciting on nursery nurse courses. It was a pleasure to observe a member of staff talk with enthusiasm to students training for her type of work and to watch the admiration and inspiration in the students as they questioned and probed into the opportunities offered at the Centre. As staff became more confident, they were invited to run workshops, act as leaders on inservice courses, and take on a supervision role with a visiting student.

The feelings of responsibility of all staff to welcome and care for visitors increased and training also gave them every opportunity to share the demands of the job with the pleasures. The increased load was shared between all staff: all were helped to feel that each one had something to offer the visitor and the trainee.

In the early years our outward looking approach had actually been a little defensive! We had initially to sell ourselves to a rather sceptical and sometimes hostile public which included colleagues in schools, other departments and other establishments. Later we came to define our community contacts with the diagram as shown in Figure 8.1.

We spent much time in creating opportunities for groups and individuals to become informed about our work. Our methods were simple, if exhausting. First there was a need to promote the recognition that the Centre was an establishment where an excellent standard and commitment to pre-school and family provision was practised. We had to create opportunities for groups and individuals to become familiar with the Centre, and we had to create situations where the work could be evaluated from outside the Centre.

(a) Outside lectures in colleges, Universities, hospitals, conferences, teachers' centre etc.

(b) Use of film, video and slides for parent evenings, social work and health visitor colleagues etc.

(c) Use of newsletters to all colleagues and community groups as well as to parents.

(d) Open evenings, many visitors from all over the country and abroad.

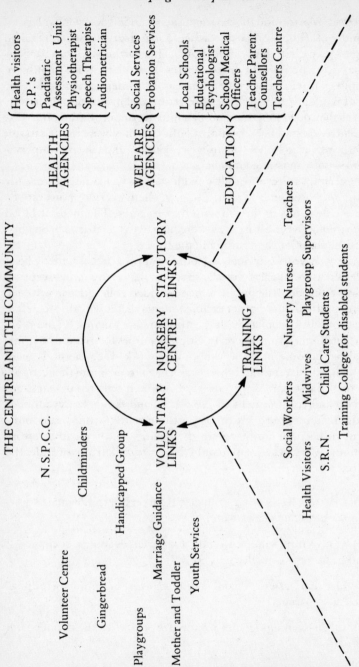

Figure 8.1 The Centre and the community

(e) Consistent interaction with professional agencies, voluntary organisations, training establishments.

(f) A warm welcome to all interested in the Centre and those seeking support and advice.

With increasing confidence and commitment we began to harness the resources in the community to maintain and develop our high standards of provision for the benefit of the children, parents and community.

Our relationships with our colleagues in other agencies had been invaluable in drawing on their expertise to supplement our own knowledge and skills. This led to more confidence between the groups in the community who also worked with families and children and led to sharing information and knowledge with trust and appreciation of each others skills. It also led to an increase and more effective use of the statutory services and voluntary agencies.

We developed a network of useful contacts through meetings, courses, and the usual professional channels. We learnt whom to contact and where and how and combined this with a persistence that seemed to produce results. We developed close links with local groups, sharing events, cross-visiting and sharing facilities and personnel.

As this commitment strengthened and developments snowballed the new work within the Centre offered a community resource which enhanced the quality of local family life. We accepted that the Centre facilities should be offered to other groups so that maximum use was made to benefit families with young children. We accepted that we must be adaptable to the changing needs of the community.

Thus considering also the shifts and holiday patterns, the large number of staff at the Centre was essential. A great deal of time was spent listening, exchanging ideas, supporting and sharing their skills and knowledge. More was expected of some staff in initiating or supporting new developments not necessarily operating in traditional school hours of 9.00 to 4.00 pm. Along with this commitment to multiple use and implicit support followed the need for discussion, planning and evaluation to establish and maintain the standards desirable. Here the role of the senior staff was of vital importance in maintaining calm working conditions which allowed all staff to express themselves to their full potential; their dedication and commitment was also essential to protect staff from exploitation.

CHAPTER 9

The transition into school

Admission to statutory schooling in Britain presents families with a number of anxieties and confusions. Admission policies are devised by the school governors with the Headteacher. The legal requirement states that children should commence school at the beginning of the term after their fifth birthday. However schools have the right to admit children as early as the year in which they will reach five years, which could mean entering an infant class just after their fourth birthday. This might be a pre-reception class, a class with five year olds, or in some schools, for example village schools and schools committed to vertical grouping, integration with children up to the age of seven years.

The young child transferring from a pre-school setting or from home will have to make many adjustments. These include a large number of children in a class, up to 32 perhaps, with only one teacher to meet all their needs. They adjust to taking their place in a large school environment; hundreds of pupils in the playground, in assembly and in the dining room. The classroom environment, access to resources and materials, a distinction between work and play, a reduction in freedom of choice and full day session may confuse and tire the nursery child who two weeks before school admission enjoyed a ratio of 1 adult to eight children, free play choices and only two and a half hours separation from home. We expect young children to adjust very quickly to these changes, often without any preparation or a gradual introduction to the changes.

Parents who have enjoyed much support and involvement in the pre-school setting may also have to adjust to the change in parental involvement policies in the infant class. They may find themselves not expected to enter a child's classroom, experience difficulties in obtaining the classteachers time to discuss the child regularly, have difficulties in understanding the school's brochure. Most importantly they will have to understand changes in curriculum and practice. The transition into school requires sensitivity and time for the child and the family if schools are to help parents support their children in an informed way. This is an important opportunity for both parents and teachers to gain an insight into each others involvement with the child and to learn from each other.

This chapter deals with one approach towards making our children's transition into the local schools as reassuring and exciting as possible, encouraging parents to continue their involvement and interest in their children's school life and to help the Centre understand the principles of continuity for the child.

The children from the Centre transferred into a number of schools in the town and several special schools in the district. There was little evidence of falling rolls at this time and the infant and primary schools nearby were very overcrowded. All children commenced statutory schooling the term after their fifth birthday. The policy caused some conflict within the Centre as our long waiting list never fell below 150 children and some children at the Centre did not start school until they were 5 years 4 months. Creating links with a number of schools was a challenge, not only due to distance but more importantly with respect to educational philosophy, continuity of care for children and parents and a commitment to the family's right and need for involvement in their children's development and education.

The Centre was situated on a shared campus with a primary school and a special school for mentally handicapped children with moderate and severe learning difficulties. Within walking distance was an infant school and by car or a short bus ride two primary schools with nursery classes and an infant school with a nursery class. The Centre accepted children referred from other agencies from within these schools' catchment areas, often because the children were under 3 years and could not be admitted to the nursery classes or because they required flexible attendance patterns, extended day support, a midday meal and holiday places. The three local nursery classes only offered five mornings or afternoon places within the school hours and terms. No meals were available. Thus some of the Centre children could not go to their neighbourhood school until after they were five years old.

There were several other special schools in the district which admitted some of our children following the decision that special schooling was more appropriate after 5. These include a physically handicapped school and a school for children with severe communication problems as well as a school for the deaf and partially hearing. During the early years changes in the local schools took place which changed the infant and junior schools into primary schools, thus increasing the number of schools to which our children could transfer.

Once our own educational practice was established on a secure footing the staff began considering ways of working more closely with primary colleagues to plan for the continuity of the children's personal progress as well as the parental support and involvement. As the Head of the Centre was a headteacher, she had access to all meetings for heads in the district and authority. She attended the local meetings in the town organised by the headteachers themselves as well as those called by the Area Education Officer, the Senior School Psychologist, the District Inspector and so on. The district meetings for heads with the Director of Education were also useful contact points at which to meet other colleagues in the primary field and to keep informed on developments in schools throughout the authority. She also attended the N.U.T. meetings and made contributions to discussions on the need for change in nursery education as well as on innovation and change in primary schools. Attending the local Trades Council meetings for a time provided an insight into life in a mining community and gave opportunities to inform other workers of children's and women's needs.

The Head had the rare chance to ensure that the local Teacher's Centre became involved in the Nursery Centre and vice versa. First the deputy head and a scale 1 teacher attended liaison committee meetings at which schools were represented. They shared the professional development issues facing teachers of young children in the primary panel meetings. A new item began to appear on the agenda of the meetings. We had raised the issue of the further professional needs of nursery nurses. The warden was faced with a challenge to involve nursery staff from our Centre and from all the other nursery establishments in many inservice events which were organised. As she was an imaginative, dynamic leader and responded by building up networks of formal and informal contacts between pre-school and primary colleagues. All centre staff were able to attend local inservice events just as they joined residential courses and workshops at the University's School of Education. Several teachers took on a two year diploma course at the local teacher training establishment which involved working and studying with primary colleagues and focusing regularly on the continuity of young children's education from 3–8 years.

At the local level our attempts to link closely with our feeder schools required time, consultation, and regular contact between the staffs. We had a policy that all staff could visit other establishments of their choice each term, during the working day. Many chose other pre-school settings, but planned visits to the feeder infant classes were vital. The Head and Matron covered for absences during these visits, and worked in the nursery. We invited our primary colleagues to reciprocate and spend time in our workplace and involve themselves in the children's play, talk with parents and observe our other activities with the community. Schools responded in different ways.

The special school on the site welcomed the liaison very much. Their assessment unit received young children for a short time and then the children were readmitted to their primary school. We developed a very trusting relationship, sharing our skills as well as information. The teacher or nursery nurse of the youngest children in the special school visited the Centre each week bringing a small group with special educational needs. They were welcomed for the afternoon and they joined in the general nursery routine, playing, sharing and being accepted by our parents. We then took groups of our children to play in their school. They had a lovely outdoor adventure play area and a warm splash pool for hydrotherapy. They also had a minibus presented by the Variety Club of Great Britain which they generously lent us for activities with our children and parents. Besides this informal sharing of learning the staff were able to share records of progress prior to some of our children transferring into the special school at 5 years of age. When we admitted young children with handicaps or delayed development or identified children with serious behaviour problems, we were grateful for the opportunity to discuss with the special school staff appropriate individual programmes and we gained personal reassurance when we felt that progress was too minimal and slow.

The special school had a well organised programme of liaison with the children's homes. We were able to contribute to the continuity of our parents' support and encouragement with their children's new school by introducing the parents to the special school staff when they worked at the Centre. The Teacher–Parent Counsellors visited the homes as well as the Centre and the schools. Our liaison with them followed through the consultations regarding children's intellectual progress, emotional and social growth and where appropriate medication and physiotherapy routines. There was, of course, some initial conflict with staff and some parents with this process of liaison. Teacher–Parent Counsellors were based with the School Psychological Service. They became involved with families with handicapped children at a very early age, referred to them by the Health Department. Homevisiting, counselling, advice on pre-school and school settings and local support groups were part of their work with parents. They also visited the pre-school and school settings and gave advice and shared information with teachers.

Some nursery staff felt insecure with other children from another establishment in their nursery base. They were understandably anxious about responsibility for discipline even though the children had their own member of staff with them. Several staff felt repulsion for visible gross handicap and were truly upset at the suggestion that they might have to go into special school. It was made quite clear that this approach was to be gradual, that no one was to be forced into the scheme of visiting the school, but that the welcome to small groups of children in our establishment would be sensitively handled with plenty of opportunity to discuss it and monitor its value. Most parents accepted this interchange and contact with handicapped children. Understandably some parents were anxious initially on the effect of the less able on their own child's progress and development. There was a fear of copying unusual behaviour and motor skills. Time was again needed to reassure and explain the reasons and advantages of the contact.

Establishing this type of liaison and professional respect with the primary and infant schools required a variety of approaches. We had to recognise some of the difficulties for our primary school colleagues. They often had large classes, no ancillary help and certainly no spare free periods. The distance for some colleagues prevented an impromptu visit during school time and the schools had busy extra curricular activities after school too. We felt that combined with these constraints, some colleagues found that they already knew and understood nursery philosophy and practice and did not need to visit during our busy day. There was also a small number of colleagues who still preferred to make their own assessment of the children's development, after starting school, and did not value other colleagues professional evaluation even though they might have worked with the child for three years, full time.

A working party of Centre staff prepared a discussion document for a staff meeting on the development of this area. The teaching staff contributed many ideas for this document. Although we shared most aspects of the Centre work, at transition it was accepted that the teachers would be in closest contact with the new school staff. This was an area of responsibility which clearly focused on the teacher's skills. She had to consult closely with each Family Group nursery nurse in her team to collate all the information for the child's profile which could be useful to a new teacher in the primary school. The profile included the child's development records, their potential and particular strengths and interests and some helpful advice about our role with the family.

Our most important aim was to work towards a smooth transition of nursery child and parents to the new school. We focused on this in several ways. In staff discussion it was vital that all staff valued and understood the need for a gradual pattern of movement from the familiar routines of the Centre into the new establishment. They in turn were ambassadors with the parents. Time was set aside for discussion with parents, questions were raised, anxieties discussed. Parents were encouraged to go to pre-admission meetings and workshops at the new school. When pre-admission visits to school were offered there was a conflict regarding the full-time children being taken to the school in the middle of their extended day. Who would take them, who would collect? Some single parents were working, another was in a wheelchair, some were very anxious about establishing new routines and relationships with the teachers at 'real school'. In some cases staff took the children for their visits. Occasionally they accompanied a parent with the child on a first visit. Teachers are often unaware of the trauma of school for parents. Parents own educational experiences combined with a distrust of 'the welfare' and their expectation of surviving on the dole and 'social' present primary schools with increasingly high barriers of poor expectations of the value of school. The vital period of transition from a pre-school group setting or directly from home offers primary schools a challenge in establishing trusting relationships with families. One of our major roles at the Centre was to bridge the gaps in the Parents' own experiences and expectations and provide a sound liaison link with the school at this stage in their child's development.

We wanted the schools to be aware of the importance of continuity of care as well as educational experiences. We had spent so much time trying to understand family need and aspirations. The conflict for us was that it could stop when the child reached 5 years of age. Our meetings with the infant teachers were sensitive to the need for confidentiality as well as for dissemination of important information regarding the child as well as the family.

We had to understand how establishments aimed to meet each child's individual needs. We welcomed an exchange in the schools' brochures for parents. These clearly set out the schools philosophy and educational aims. They described the school curriculum, the teaching methods, the extra curricular activities and the involvement of parents.

To overcome the problems of school staff not being able to visit us during the day we embarked on making a video film of our approach to the children's all round development. The Teacher's Centre Warden provided the expertise with the video camera. Each team of staff planned their own contribution to the film. The earliest work with the under threes was as important as the older children's programme. The film was then edited and a small information sheet produced with some guidance to the value of these early experiences in the film sequences, see Appendix 1 – Notes with a video film on Life at the Centre.

A pattern of consultation meetings began to emerge. At each half term infant teams were invited to tea at the Centre. The three teachers would then share with the infant staff a wide ranging discussion on the children about to begin pre-admission visits at the school. Of course, the staff often knew our children because of their older siblings in school. They were also working with the same parents in many cases. Following these meetings teachers made an appointment with the family of each child about to leave, fitting in with family convenience, and again the extra help of the Head and Matron in the nursery released the teachers for these essential meetings. Each family was then involved in discussing their child's progress during their stay at the Centre and informed of the assessment of their child's stage of development. They knew that meetings were in progress between the schools and were pleased to be involved and aware of the sort of shared information being exchanged.

We then held a wine and cheese evening and invited the school's staff to join us to view the film. Health visitors and social workers also attended and the key workers with the handicapped children, the NSPCC and the childcare teachers at the comprehensive school. They were able to take the film notes away for future use in their schools and offices.

Besides encouraging parents with visits to the new schools we became involved in taking our older children 'into school'. In the primary school on the same campus we were timetabled to use their lovely carpeted hall each week; both teachers would take the older children in small groups to use the climbing and agility apparatus. Children gained confidence in the school setting, experience of changing clothes for active physical education and regular contact with the Headmaster and passing staff. Nearer the transfer to school the children joined an infant class in 'movement' or music lessons or a story time. Then they were left in the infant class for a session to draw or paint or handle now familiar play apparatus. Our close proximity to the school made all the easier this type of cooperation.

It was not easy to work in this way with the further distanced schools. The Head established the first contact by an informal meeting with the Headteacher. Gradually regular visits by a nursery nurse or teacher with children were established with the gradual withdrawal of the Centre staff for the session. It was a crucial link, developed by pressure, from the Centre. Transport was always available, the Head driving a member of staff and children to the school concerned, leaving them and going back to make up for the absent member of staff and then returning later to collect them all. The Deputies and Matron contributed to this ferrying programme when necessary.

As children returned to the Centre from their visits, much was made of their experience by the staff. Children spilled over with exciting anecdotes and showed their paintings and drawings completed in the 'big school'. The cook, the cleaner, the laundry assistant and the clerical assistant all followed through the excitement, encouragement and praise. As they saw children and their parents in their work about the Centre, they would stop and enquire about the visits and praise the child and reassure the parents – they all had children who had gone through the town's schools or were attending them too. They were able to give personal reassurance through their contacts as parents which enhanced our liaison links and added an important extra dimension.

It was hard work establishing the links with so many schools but gradually we felt that a sound cooperative approach was developing. There was still much to develop. We wanted to attend school staff meetings to make contributions to curriculum planning so that our primary colleagues would build on the foundation of essential learning experiences offered at the Centre. We also wanted infant colleagues to join our discussions on extending our able children, providing for children well over 5 years of age. We needed more constructive discussion on how they valued our contribution to prepare children for school. We needed a great deal of sensitive exchange of ideas here as we did not belong to the school of thought which focused on nurseries being in existence to prepare children to go to the toilet unaided at school, or to answer the register, to sit quietly and do as they were told or to hang up their coats and do their shoes up. We were working with a commitment towards our children moving forward confidently from babyhood towards an articulate motivated pupil status. William van de Eyken describes this phase as leading towards the development of the 'competent child, acknowledging the child's problem solving ability and their capacity for applied intelligence, using their enhancing environment to learn about their own world'.

This stage of development, however, would be the next challenge for Centre staff.

CHAPTER 10

Innovation often means isolation – some thoughts for the future

The White Paper, *Education, A Framework for Expansion*, published in 1972, set the pattern for the development of nursery education. It recommended that the future pattern would be increasingly part-time provision for children aged 3–5years, based in nursery units in primary and infant school. By the 1980s, those authorities with a commitment to nursery expansion have implemented these expectations. There has been a decline in creating nursery schools, though a few authorities have experimented with Nursery Centres. Changes in admission to statutory schooling affected by falling rolls and increased spare accommodation in schools is making a different impact on nursery provision. Four year olds are increasingly attending school full-time without the facilities and resources or staff trained to meet their needs. Schools are also operating one year intake at the beginning of a school year, rather than new admissions each term. The Child Health and Education Study in Bristol reveals that in North and Northwest regions 82 per cent and 63.9 per cent respectively and in Wales 76.5 per cent for children are in this category.

The trend therefore continues towards the traditional educational bias of school rather than a new look at the changing lives of families with young children who require longer or more flexible day care patterns, school holiday provision, facilities for parents or improved cooperation between the Health, Social Services and Education Departments.

The subtle changes in teacher training towards an even more academic approach with little change in considering the needs of parents in their child's education is not preparing our teachers of the future towards a multidisciplinary and community approach towards early childhood education.

Nursery nurse training continues to prepare 16–18 year olds for the challenge of pre-school work, although there was much evidence in the contributions made to the panel of enquiry reviewing the future of nursery nursing that this age group was too young. It continues to attract mostly young white women. It also continues to fail to raise the image of this profession from a solely caring, nanny image in its most traditional sense to a highly informed, articulate pre-school worker able to take on the challenges of the varying provision. There is still little opportunity for promotion or further professional inservice training.

During the first ten years of operation the Kirkby nursery centre staff closely examined existing day care and education practice, considered new challenges to adapt and meet the community needs and spent considerable time trying to equip themselves with the necessary skills and understanding to reduce the conflict and stress and widen the opportunities for personal growth, professional responsibility and real job satisfaction. With hindsight we can give some guidance to agencies considering creating a more flexible pre-school institution on the needs of the staff, the needs of parents and the wide ranging needs of young children.

During the early years there was considerable conflict of personalities, of philosophy, of job role and responsibility and of strategies for acquiring the necessary skills for the changes and demands made on the staff.

The selection of suitable staff was crucial. A variety of skills and experience was essential. The expectation to work with adults as well as children must focus selection partly on maturity, on flexible attitudes and a willingness to learn and share in a team situation. There was a need for staff to communicate effectively, to value the contributions of other disciplines to the centre's development and to establish and maintain these links which lay aside professional barriers and fostered trust, respect and tolerance. Staff personality was as important as their professional training. They had to be approachable, diplomatic, and confident in their own role and with their own skills. Observation and assessment skills were vital. Empathy with parents and an expectation of parental partnership in the centre was essential. Counselling, delegation and organisation were important personal skills.

It is important to acknowledge the training of early childhood staff. Teaching and nursery nursing provide essential knowledge and skills for the newly trained nursery staff, in working with children. However, health visiting and social work skills and expertise are increasingly needed in the pre-school institution if the whole child's developmental needs are to be met. The community education programme requires other skills not yet included in nursery staff initial training. The presence of an all female, all white staff presents challenges when trying to combat racism and sexism in the pre-school setting. We also need to acknowledge the tremendous resources of the voluntary workers particularly those in playgroups, adventure playschemes, one o'clock clubs, PHAB clubs and gateway clubs for the handicapped and in childminding schemes. The nursery centre could offer new opportunities for a wider range of staff, with job sharing and other flexible arrangements to enrich the young child's world, support family life and broaden nursery staff perspectives.

It was interesting to note that neither the Head, the Matron or the Deputy Head or the Deputy Matron had followed traditional patterns of professional development and promotion. Between them they brought perspectives from other pre-school settings to the centre. One had been a Social Services playgroups and Childminder Adviser. Another had been a peripatetic playgroup leader, employed by Social Services to support new playgroups. One had been a childminder, running her own small group in her home. Another had worked abroad teaching English to pre-school children and lived in a community with no other English residents. Several nursery nurses had worked in hospitals in baby and premature baby units as well as on the wards. One of the teachers had had experience as an Area Organiser for the Pre-school Playgroup Association and several staff had tutored courses at Adult Education classes, in particular for playgroup parents on the value of play and childrens development. These were all useful experiences and insights into other approaches to working with young children and families.

What was needed in the early years and at regular intervals onwards were relevant inservice events followed up by an evaluation of further training needs to be met jointly by both departments. There was so much expertise to draw in from the Inspectorate and Advisory Service in Education and the Training Department of Social Services. This was an oppportunity sadly missed. Whatever induction was available to new staff was designed by the centre staff. The Head teacher's induction followed the primary Heads' pattern. This of course was useful and essential in establishing the links with administrators at County Hall, but did not examine the inter-departmental resources in the district essential for the centre to reach its full potential.

Primary schools were able to close once a year for an inservice training day to give the whole staff a full day to consider an aspect of their work in depth. We were grateful for the opportunity to benefit from this type of inservice day. This is essential provision for the future too. Time should be allocated each year for inservice work and the Training and Inspectorate Advisory Service should be heavily involved in its planning with the staff, see Appendix Two, Inservice Training –a brief encounter.

As there was so much change in direction, in job role, and in expected skills the staff needed a formal supervision session time-tabled regularly to meet with the Head to discuss their work, their aspirations and anxieties, their training needs and their future career prospects. Such personal sessions should have been built into the review procedures for the Centre.

The main form of appraisal of the Centre's work was the termly report prepared jointly for the Management Committee which was modelled on a primary school committee. This was useful as it gave the Head and Matron an opportunity to review together the progress being made, the problems requiring consideration and the improve-ments that would enhance Centre life. The managers were represen-tatives of the County Council, District Council, Area Office, the parents and the staff. In recognition of our connections with Social Services an officer was invited to attend these meetings. The meet-ings were supportive and we were most fortunate to receive from this committee the personal help, the positive advice and unceasing support for the many new directions in which the Centre was moving.

During this period of innovation, however, there was a corres-ponding period of financial constraint nationally and locally. Budgets were being reduced, inservice events limited, teachers' centres closed, with redundancies and redeployment of nursery nurses in nurseries and in schools. Advisers who retired or moved were not replaced. Opportunities for secondment disappeared.

The Centres became particularly isolated at this time. The local nursery classes were plunged into a period of restricted practice as the staff ratios were altered to 1 adult to 20 children which made for a very difficult relationship with the Centres which continued with a staffing ratio of 1–5. Our Centre received 60 children each day with all the support of the high ratios of staff to work with children and parents and other agencies. The 60 place classes in the primary schools had 3 staff. Centre staff and parents joined the protest marches and attended the days of action to draw attention to our concern for the reduction of staffing and services, but we had been miraculously protected. Relationship problems with colleagues in the primary sector obviously occurred. Many headteachers and classteachers felt that nurseries should be closed so that the reduced resources were all available in the statutory sector. An old rallying call began to rattle around Kirkby that children should be at home with their mothers and that nurseries were not only expensive but unnecessary. Several primary heads admitted at meetings that they had not wanted their nursery classes but had had them forced on them during the period of growth.

When Centre staff attended any of the few courses available for nursery staff, care and sensitivity for the awful difficulties their colleagues in nursery classes were experiencing had to be exercised. This often influenced staff to reject meetings and contact with these other colleagues because our working situations were so grossly different.

These financial constraints were being experienced in many parts of the country of course. For some years the senior centre staff had created their own self help group nationally. Heads and Matrons had been meeting two or three times a year in other centres to explore their differences, praise their achievements and learn from each other. These meetings were invaluable. We would drive to Coventry or Bolton or Birmingham and spend a day just talking and listening and laughing together, returning refreshed and comforted and very important, reassured and strong. It was at this difficult time of developing isolation within the pre-school services that we decided to establish a Nursery Centre Association. All staff could join and working parties were created to consider constitutions, courses and conferences. The first National Conference was held at Thomas Coram Children's Centre in London. We borrowed the neighbouring school's minibus and eleven centre staff set off at 6 a.m. one Saturday for the Big City. Only the Head had ever been to London, so the trip offered more than a chance to see another centre and talk with other colleagues.

That day was magical. Eleven exhausted women returned at 4 a.m. the following morning having accomplished a marathon London experience. The conference had excellent speakers and workshops. Staff met others struggling with far more difficulties than we were. Nursery nurses as well as teachers shared their experiences and thoughts and all began to be aware that they were part of a real team approach towards work. After the conference, we tried the Underground, Leicester Square, Trafalgar Square, Horse Guards Parade, Westminster, St James and finally Buckingham Palace. Teetering exhaustedly into Victoria there was a lovely meal followed by the Theatre. This event did a great deal for staff morale. It brought the group closer and clarified the support and care we gave each other. Most importantly it reduced the isolation of working in a new type of provision, unaware that there were groups of other staff struggling and meeting the challenges that we were.

In many areas of our nursery work we had begun to change some of the rigid divisions between care and education philosophies practiced in many state day nurseries and nursery classes and schools. Our concern for families as well as for young children required bridge building between the professions, between parents and between administrators. The wider expectation of linking pre-school education with continuing education for parents and women in particular required flexible liaison patterns to establish health, education, social and recreation networks in the centre and the community.

It is a sad fact that in periods of economic stringency, early childhood education and day care are considered a luxury. In our experience this is totally opposite to the reality for a community experiencing industrial and economic recession. We learned that nursery provision is highly desirable for all children and a necessity for most. In high quality provision the nursery should complement positively the benefits and strengths of a favourable physical, familiar and community environment: it is necessary because many children do not enjoy those benefits.

Unfortunately there is renewed enthusiasm for low cost provision, for selection, and means tested provision, for cuts in quality and the amount of public provision for the education and care of young children. However, the development of the Nursery Centre gave us inspiration and confidence to share with those interested our thoughts for future growth.

Throughout this book I have tried to identify quality practice in daycare and early childcare education. I would suggest that the following criteria are critical ideals:

1 The nursery should be community based, within easy walking distance for parents and staff who may need to home visit, offering flexible hours and open throughout the year.

2 It should be generously staffed, so that children enjoy small groups and a great deal of individual attention and parents can be supported and involved.

3 Unions and management should work closely to ensure that all staff receive salaries which reflect the changing demands and expectations of this development in pre-school provision. Adequate holidays should be offered to reduce ill-health, tiredness, and stress well documented in day care research. The National Nursery Centres Association recommend, not less than 8 weeks and ideally 10 weeks leave.

4 There should be adequate inservice training and support to establish and maintain the high quality of staff, which should encourage a stability essential to quality day care and education.

5 Ideally there should be medical and welfare support services available in or very near the Centre, for the convenience of the families and to foster easy liaison and cooperation between agencies.

6 There should be generous provision for parent representation at management level to promote true parent participation.

7 There should be generous facilities throughout the Centre for parents.

8 The environment should be planned to foster maximum flexibility and used to meet the needs of the children, parents, staff and community.

9 It must be free to all, with democratic admission criteria so that no family is ineligible to make use of its facilities.

Thus the nursery centre should incorporate all the advantages and avoid the disadvantages of the usual segregated pattern of care and education. It should reduce conflict between parents and professionals and create community cooperation to maximise our common resources for the benefit of the young child and the family.

This account has described one approach to the problem; a step forward in new directions, sometimes stumbling, increasingly surefooted. To take the experience further our pre-school establishments now need to look more closely at changing the stereotypes in early childcare. We must look at reducing sex stereotyping in staffing, in educational practice, and in parental expectations. If we truly believe that early childhood is the most formative period, new approaches to equality of opportunity must be tackled. Our attitudes to race and culture provide new conflicts and challenges. Changes in our provision and practice must reflect our multi-cultural society. Too much time has been wasted in conflict between nursery nurse and nursery teacher, playgroup versus nursery education, women's right to work versus the woman's place is in the home. If we are not careful the next phase will be white worker versus black, white women versus black women. What we want is parent, professional, volunteer, administrator, academic and trainer working cooperatively towards a unified pre-school service which is flexible, free and a wonderful place to work regardless of age, colour or gender.

Appendix One: Notes with a video film on life at the Centre

1 A single father (with 4 children) and a single mother (with three children) redecorating wall in Baby Den. Children helping.
   – a lovely domestic scene rarely experienced by day care children.

2 Matron and a 2 year old – individual attention.
   – Different shape and size containers, early concept development.
   – Ordering objects, eg, all shells in one box.
   – matching and fitting lids to boxes.
   – listening to sounds, touching textures stuck to base of tin.
   – conversation, language development.

3 Nursery Nurse and 2 year olds.
   – sorting and matching textured squares, early concept development.
   – extended concentration at activity.
   – value of adult involved.
   – conversation, language development.

4 Visiting Social Worker and 2 year old.
   – a welcome male figure in a female world.
   – a quiet few minutes in a busy playroom, a warm lap, a cuddle.

5 Nursery Nurse and group of 2 year olds.
   - looking at and selecting items from a shopping bag.
   - smelling, touching, tasting, listening, observing.
   - plenty of language input from adult.
   - taking turns, sharing.

6 Deputy Matron and 2 year old suffering from Brittle Bone Disease and poor speech.
   - discussing pictures, matching shapes, concentrating, manipulating objects.
   - encouragement, praise.

7 Babies outing. Essential for day care children confined to an institution.

8 Staff in Baby Den discussing a child about to leave the Den to join a Family Group in the main nursery.
   - assessing child's all round development, notes for new nursery nurse.
   - student encouraged to contribute to team discussion.
   - discussing change in routine etc.
   - information for the teacher.

9 Working with the 3–5 year olds.
   - older children arriving, parents welcome, a flexible start to the session.

10 Nursery Nurse and group of children in home corner.
   - domestic play, social development, sharing, talking etc.
   - linking home with school, importance of adult involvement.
   - extending the language.

11 Teacher and child aged 5 years.
   - sorting different shapes, colours and size beads.
   - matching, counting and discussing.

12 Nursery Nurse and Family Group (some full day care with some part-time children) at a cooking activity.
   - domestic reality.
   - measuring, counting, discussing, tasting.
   - sharing, taking turns.
   - complex actions, creaming, whisking, cracking eggs, good control.

- extended concentration and attention.
- thorough enjoyment of the activity and the group together-
  ness.

13 Nursery Nurse and Family Group – story time in Quiet Den.
   - quiet reflective time in a busy day.
   - listening, observing, concentrating
   - following a sequence in a story, new vocabulary and ideas.
   - empathy with the characters in story.

14 Class singing session with staff and mother helpers.

15 Teacher preparing group of older children for visit to market.
   - looking, listening, discussing, anticipating, questioning,
     recalling.

16 Teacher and four mothers preparing to join the rota of helpers.
   - share anxiety, reassure each other, prepare and discuss
     expectations.

17 Shy new mother helper, talking, playing involved.

18 Experienced mother helper with group of children (tasting
   foods)
   - tasting, sharing, guessing, remembering and talking.
   - thoroughly enjoying the activity.
   - increased confidence of mother, important addition to staff
     skills.

19 Teacher and group of rising fives (making a fresh fruit salad)
   - handling new fruits, new tastes, textures, colours, shapes.
   - difficult new skills with tools, knives, squeezer.
   - praise encouragement, concentration and deep interest.
   - early maths, halves and quarters etc.
   - new vocabulary, conversation.
   - importance of adult involvement and interest in other mat-
     ters.

20 Woodwork with teacher nearby.
   - concentration, skills, creative.
   - observing other children, taking turns.

21 Nursery Nurse and Family Group – colour display.
   - discussing objects, identifying colours, taking turns.

22 Teacher at water trolley.
   - observing, discussing, concentrating, identifying colours.
   - selecting size and shape.

23 Mother helper and group game.
   - identifying and matching pictures.
   - talking, taking turns, completing task.

24 Teacher and 4 year old with speech difficulties, following up speech therapist advice.
   - labelling objects, help with sounds.
   - encouraging concentration.
   - conversation – one to one.

25 Group singing game.
   - coping with formal group.
   - following instructions.
   - remembering words.
   - quality of movement and volume of sounds.
   - enjoying the activity.

26 Two full-time teachers discussing with the part-time teacher the children leaving to attend primary school.
   - assessing development at transfer.
   - preparing to meet their colleagues in the Infant Departments with their development records.
   - trying to foster continuity.
   - recognising the part-time teacher's contribution to the child's progress.

Appendix Two: Inservice training – a brief encounter

Following the exciting years at the Centre I joined the Inspector and Advisory Service of the local education department. My experience had highlighted that an effective inservice training programme was a powerful component in change and innovation. All the learning and experience at the Centre influenced an attempt to produce an increased awareness in the Primary Phase and across pre-school agencies of the exciting and necessary changes in curriculum development, parental involvement and professional fulfilment that are attainable in a cooperative approach towards early childhood education.

There are many training resources available to the local authority. Most education departments have an inservice budget for teachers. Nursery nurses work in a team, a partnership with teaching colleagues. It is essential to recognise that this professional group working with young children should be included in planning for the post-qualifying local based courses. Inservice events can be offered in a variety of ways. There are school based courses held in an establishment with the staff involved in the planning having identified their needs. Schools can be closed for a day each year for a study day together which is often used as a springboard for further work in the term after school hours. A pyramid of schools may opt to close and share a study day, enabling nursery staff to debate and share issues with primary and secondary colleagues. In Nottinghamshire we experimented with Nursery Study Days. We closed groups of nursery classes and schools for a day to share early years' issues. Many colleagues feared separation from the primary phase proper. However just as many nursery colleagues valued these events greatly having attended courses aimed essentially at upper primary practice. Headteachers, nursery teachers, nursery nurses and infant colleagues met with the Teachers' Centre Warden and the Early Years Inspector to plan the events, take responsibility for groupwork, workshops and organisation, and most important, the evaluation of the events. These evaluations by course members became the core for further inservice.

Our early attempts to offer more effective inservice training became enriched by inviting our local playgroup, childminders and day nursery colleagues to join us, make contributions and share our resources. Gradually parents were involved in the events as we considered parent issues, transition into nursery and first school and so on. As our courses focused on children with special needs it was important to involve colleagues in special education, Area Health and the School Psychological Service as well as other departments and the voluntary agencies, to share their skills and knowledge and broaden the often insular based practice. The many and varied resources available to the Education Department seem to point the way forward in extending and using such resources across the agencies to benefit the wide range of staff working with young children in a community.

Links between the Inspection and Advisory Service with the Colleges of Further and Higher Education, the Polytechnics and the University provide opportunities to link and liaise with the classroom practitioner to influence change in further professional courses. These colleges are not only centres of inservice for teachers, but also for nursery nurses, social work and day care staff, health visitors, community workers and so on. Links in funding with the Workers Education Association and other voluntary agencies can also draw together other imaginative and innovative colleagues prepared to share issues and resources to maximise the benefits to a wider audience.

Some simple examples illustrate the potential of a cooperative approach towards an interdisciplinary inservice programme for early years' staff.

As the playgroup movement has such a successful history of involving parents in their children's education, I approached the

Regional Training and Development Officer for the Pre-school Playgroups Association to discuss sharing that expertise with primary school staff. Following this discussion, a meeting was arranged with three schools in a pilot scheme focused on helping parents understand and value play in the early years in school. The Head-teachers, school staff and P.P.A. course tutors with funds from the W.E.A. transferred from education, set up 'doorstep' courses for parents in spare school accommodation. This enabled 15 parents in each nursery in the schools to enjoy an eight week workshop, very practically based, on play. Close involvement of school staff in this scheme enabled us to prepare a rationale for a Curriculum Development scheme whereby a bid for funds for a two year project was successful. A deputy head of an infant school with a nursery was seconded for two years to set up other schemes in schools to give teachers skills in adult education, organising more effective parent evenings and workshops on many aspects of the curriculum. The working party set up to support this colleague included P.P.A. and Health Education, the University and the Inspectorate.

A practical approach to setting up appropriate inservice training for nursery school and day nursery staff should be one of the most easily accomplished tasks in a local authority. Training Officers in Social Services and the Inspectors in Education are employed by the same local authority. Budgets could so easily be shared on certain aspects of training. We successfully organised two residential experiences for day nursery and school staff, by setting up a joint planning group of officers and nursery staff. One event focused on parental support and involvement and the other on children with special needs. These events were so successful – and why not? Colleagues working and living together for three days, debating common issues, sharing and overlapping experiences and being exposed to new ideas were involved in the planning, the group leadership and the evaluation of these events. Very valuable contributions were also made on both these courses by the voluntary agencies and Health staff. Staff put their own work into perspective, many were introduced to colleagues in their community outside the school system to whom they could turn for guidance and support.

Another example of cooperation which can enrich and extend inservice training is the close involvement of Inspectors and Training

Officers with the Further Education Colleges which provide nursery nurse training. College staff, officers and the nursery staff at the grass roots in a shared training experience is a powerful element for change in practice. The reality of modern nursery work with its wider implications for more skills to work with adults and other agencies must be recognised in the colleges to prepare nursery staff for the challenge of early childhood care and education.

The natural development of low cost, low key integration of many local inservice events was to look at the potential for a Regional approach to this development. Teachers, social work staff, health visitors, and special needs staff have access to a host of post qualifying training with further degrees and diplomas. Yet much of the work done in the pre-school field is supported by the voluntary sector, struggling on sparse budgets, relying on grants from the local Education and Social Services departments. These organisations have demonstrated a high commitment and gained valuable experiences which should be shared with their statutory colleagues, and vice versa.

It is possible to challenge the conflict in the pre-school services by working positively through inservice training to draw all the sectors closer to understand their contribution to the under fives and their families. Respect and understanding challenge myth and ignorance and provide a strong base for bridge building across the departments and agencies.

The D.E.S. Regional course network is a flexible ally in providing a practical approach towards an interdisciplinary training course. Teachers, trainers, voluntary agencies, health staff, day care and social work staff can all contribute to the planning group with an impartial evaluator observing and reporting on the success of the course. This group can collectively organise courses tailor-made for a range of disciplines because they are also the consumer. Finances for school staff are fairly easily available in most local authorities. Training Departments in health and Social Services can identify their staffs needs and budget effectively to ensure participation in this type of course. Written information and requests from the planning group to the voluntary agencies requesting support and sponsorship for their members has proved satisfactory. In one such event the Social Services Committee sponsored local childminders and a county councillor to attend. Once established in a region, departments and agencies can budget annually for this course, particularly if the officers and staff have been involved in the planning.

The logical conclusion to this development is to create a regional and interdisciplinary training panel to organise regular events. We found that the Nottinghamshire staff were very favourably situated with both the University and the Poly in the county. It was essential to share this benefit out in the rural districts and other counties. Thus efforts were made to involve the colleges of further and higher education and the teacher centres. The formation of a regional panel brought many trainers together from the statutory and voluntary sectors as well as the college lecturers. The richness of this variety should not only provide more effective inservice events but would hopefully influence initial training courses and offer future generations of pre-school workers a realistic training which matches the challenges of the changes in pre-school work.

Throughout the wide area of initial and further training there is one principle which should not be ignored, the core of excellent practice and expertise in the field. Training cannot be seen to be experts in seats of learning offering pearls of wisdom. The reality of effective pre-school provision is the close cooperation of the worker in the community with the family and the child and all the other agencies to ensure the child reaches its full potential. Our trainers must draw on the wide ranging expertise out in the schools, the day care centres, the playgroups, the community and the home. The move towards a highly academic teacher force without recognising the changing role of the teacher of young children is very questionable. At a D.E.S. Regional course in Nottingham attended by many disciplines working with the pre-school child and the family, it was very strongly recommended that the changing direction in the early years be recognised in the training of nursery staff. There is a need for in depth consideration of the effect of family life on young children, the needs of parents, the partnership of parents with the professionals in their child's education. Communication skills in working with a wide range of adults and agencies was a key issue of concern. Assessment and evaluation skills, particularly in relation to children with special needs and child abuse were highlighted. Tackling issues such as sexism and racism in the curriculum and in practice were recognised as issues that were deeply important in effecting change in our society.

Integrating approaches to the care and education of young

children is now of prime importance if we are to meet the needs of families and reduce educational disadvantages. It is urgently appropriate to seek ways of drawing the wide ranging pre-school services closer together under one directorate, integrating the expertise and skills, enriching established practice and moving towards a more equal start for all our children in the future.

Notes and References

1 Conflicts in the education and care of the pre-school child

References and further reading

Blackstone, T. (1971). *Fair Start: the provision of preschool education*, London: Allen Lane.

Bone, M. (1977). *Preschool Children and the need for daycare*, London: HMSO.

Central Advisory Council for Education, (1967), *Children and their Primary Schools*, London: HMSO.

Committee on Local Authority and Allied Personal Social Services, (1968) London: HMSO.

DES, (1972), *Education – a framework for expansion*, London: HMSO.

DHSS, (1976), *Low cost provision for the Under Fives*, London: DHSS.

Conference Papers at the Sunningdale Conference 9–10 January 1976.

Halsey, A. H., (1972), *EPA – Problems and Policies*, Vol 1 DES.

Hughes, M., Mayall, B., Moss, P., Perry, J., Petrie, P., and Pinkerton, G. (1980), *Nurseries Now*, Pelican.

Jackson, B., (1976), 'Childminding' a breakthrough point in the cycle of deprivation' in *Low Cost Day Care Provision for Under Fives*, London: DHSS.

Jackson, B., Jackson, S., (1979), *Childminder – a study in action research*, London: Routledge and Kegan Paul.

McMillan, M., (1930), *The Nursery School*, Dent.

Midwinter, E., (1974), *Preschool Priorities*, London: Wardlock.

Pringle, Mia Kelmer and Naidoo, S., (1975), *Early childcare in Britain*, London: Gordon & Breach.

NALGO, (19   ), 'Workplace Nurseries – a negotiating kit', Pub NALGO, 1 Mabledon Place.

NUT, (1977), 'Needs of Under Fives'. Report for Members.

TUC, (1976), 'The Under Fives – report of a working party', TUC Congress, Congers House.

2   Kirkby Nursery Centre – changing attitudes, roles and expectations

References and further reading

Blackstone, T., (1973), *Education and daycare for young children in need*, London: Bedford Square Press.

Clift, P., Cleave, S., Griffin, M., (1980), *The aims, role and deployment of staff in the nursery*, Slough: National Foundation for Educational Research, NFER.

Fein, F., Clark Stewart, A., (1973), *Daycare in context*, New York: Wiley.

Ferri, E., Birchall, D., Gingell, V., Gipps, C., (1981), *Combined Nursery Centres*, London: MacMillan.

3   Communications – a framework for development

References and further reading

Argyle, M., (1974), *The social psychology of work*, Harmondsworth Middx: Penguin.

Cartwright, D. and Zander, A., (1968), Group Dynamics, London: Tavistock Publications.

Ferri, E., Birchall, D., Gingell, V., Gipps, C., (1981), *Combined Nursery Centres,* London: MacMillan.

4 First impressions: crises, stresses and small successes

References and further reading

DHSS/DES Circular (1978), *Coordinating Services for children under five* LASSL/78/1 HMSO.
DHSS (1976), *Low cost provision for Under Fives*, DHSS/DES.
TUC (1976), Report of the Working Party on the Under Fives, TUC Congress House.
Kitzinger, S., (1978), *Women as Mothers*, Glasgow: Collins.
Kempe, R., Kemp, C. H., (1978), *Child Abuse,* Glasgow, Fontana.
Renvoize, J., (1974), *Children in Danger*, Harmondsworth Middx: Pelican.
Ross, Mitchell, (1975), *Depression*, Harmondsworth Middx: Pelican.
Rutter, M., (1972), *Maternal Deprivation reassessed*, Harmondsworth Middx: Penguin.
Wolff, Sula, (1969), *Children under stress*, Harmondsworth Middx: Pelican.

5 Building blocks – creating the right environment and relationships

References and further reading

DES, (1981), *Underfives, a programme of research*, A Handbook by Under Fives, Research Dissemination Group, HMSO.
DHSS, (1984), Service for under fives from Ethnic Minority Communities, London: HMSO.
Garland, C., White, S., (1980), *Children and Day Nurseries*, London: Grant McIntyre.

6 Early childhood education

References

Addison Wesley, (1978), *Early Mathematical Experiences* Set of guides, Published Schools Council.

Bruner, J. (1980), *Under Fives in Britain*, London: Grant McIntyre.

(1972), Nuffield Mathematical Teaching Project, Checking Up I+II. Pub. for Nuffield Foundation by W. & R. Chambers & John Murray, London.

Cicirelli, V. G., Granger, R. L. *et al.*, (1969), *The Impact of Headstart: an evaluation of the effects of Headstart on Children's cognitive and affective development*, Westinghouse Learning Corporation and Ohio University.

Choat, E., (1973), *Preschool Maths*, London: Wardlock.

Clift, P., Cleave, S., Griffin, M., (1980), *Aims, role and deployment of staff in the nursery*, Slough: NFER.

Donaldson, Margaret, (1978), *Children's Minds*, Glasgow: Fontana.

Halsey, A. H., (ed.), (1972), Educational Priority vol 1, EPA Problem and Policies, London: HMSO.

Matthews, G., (ed.), (1972), *Mathematics through School*, London: Pub. John Murray.

McMillan, M., (1919), *The Camp School*, London: Allen and Unwin.

McMillan, M., (1930), *The Nursery School*, London: Dent.

Piaget, J., (1926), *The Language and Thought of the Child*, London: Routledge and Kegan Paul.

Piaget, J., (1952), *The Child's Conception of Numbers*, London: Routledge and Kegan Paul.

Piaget, J., (1958), *The Child's Construction of Reality*, London: Routledge and Kegan Paul.

Plowden Report, (1967), Central Advisory Council for Education, *Children and their Primary Schools*, HMSO.

Sylva, K., Roy, C., Pointer, M., *Childwatching at Playgroup and Nursery School*, London: Grant McIntyre.

Tough, J., (1976), *Listening to Children Talking, A Guide to the Appraisal of Children's Use of Language*, London: Wardlock.

Tough, J., (1977), *The Development of Meaning*, London: Allen and Unwin.

Tough, J., (1977), *Talking and Learning, a Guide for fostering communication skills in the Nursery and Infant School*, London: Wardlock.

Weikart, D., Epstein, A., Schweinhart, L., Bond, J., (1978), *The Ypsilanti Preschool Curriculum Demonstration Project*, High/Scope.

7 Parental Involvement – the changing needs of families with young children

References

Brown, G., Bhrolchain, M. and Harris, T., (1975), *Social Class and Psychiatric Disturbance among women in an urban population*, Sociology 9, 225–254.

Further Reading

Atkins, J., and Bastiani, J., (1985), *Preparing Teachers to work with parents, A Survey of Initial Training*, Nottingham University School of Education.

Pugh, G., De'ath, E., (1984), *The Needs of Parents*, London: Mac-Millan.

Smith, T., (1980), *Parents and Preschool*, London: Grant McIntyre.

Tizard, B., *et al.*, (1981), *Involving Parents in Nursery and Infant Schools*, London: Grant McIntyre.

9 The transition into school

Further reading

Chazan, M., Laing, A. F., Shackleton Bailey and Glenys Jones (1980), *Some of Our Children*, London: Open Books.

Cleave, S., Jowett, S. and Bate, M., (1982), *And so to School*, Windsor: NFER.

Louis Legrand, (1978), 'Educational Research on new developments in Primary Education', Council of Europe, NFER.

Pugh, G., De'ath, E., (1984), *Needs of Parents*, London: MacMillan.

Tizard, B., Mortimore, J., Burchell, B., (1981), *Involving parents in Nursery and Infant schools*, London: Grant McIntyre.

Van der Eyken, W., (1982), *The education of three to eight year olds in Europe in the eighties*, NFER, Nelson.

10 Innovation often means isolation – some thought for the future

References and further reading

Bastiani, J., (1983), (Coordinator) *Teacher–Parent Interviews, Some materials for teachers*, Nottingham University.

Bastiani, J., Aikin, J. (1985), *Preparing teachers to work with parents*, Nottingham University.

Ferri, E., Birchall, D., Gingell, V. and Gipps, C. (1981), *Combined Nursery Centres*, London: MacMillan.

Osborn, A., Butler, N., and Morris, A. (1984), *The Social life of Britains five year olds – a report of Child Health and Education Study*, London: Routledge and Kegan Paul.

Nursery Nursing, Published NNEB Board, Argyle House, 29–31 Euston Rd, London NW1.